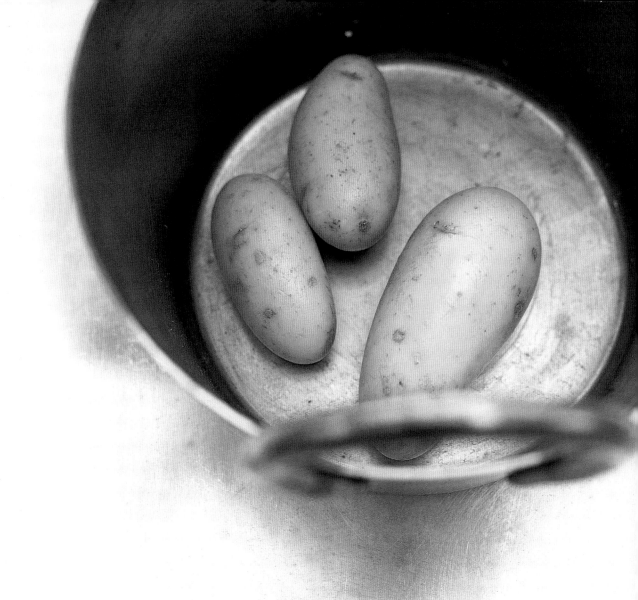

a PASSION
for POTATOES

a passion for potatoes

Paul Gayler

with photography by Gus Filgate

THE LYONS PRESS
Guilford, Connecticut

An Imprint of The Globe Pequot Press

to my wife, anita, and to my
Late mothers, Lilian and joyce

First Lyons Press edition, 2001

First published in Great Britain in 2001 by Kyle Cathie Limited

Text copyright © 2001 by Paul Gayler
Photography copyright © 2001 by Gus Filgate

The Lyons Press is an imprint of The Globe Pequot Press.

Printed in Singapore

ISBN 1-58574-463-8

10 9 8 7 6 5 4 3 2 1

The Library of Congress Cataloguing-in-Publication Data is available on file.

contents

INTRODUCTION

What other vegetable evokes such nostalgic feelings as the potato? It is part and parcel of my childhood memories – roast potatoes for Sunday lunch; baked potatoes thrown on the fire on Guy Fawkes Night; a midweek supper of sausage and mash; and, of course, fish and chips on a Friday. My particular passion was mashed potatoes with salad dressing, which I have to admit I still enjoy but I like to feel that my tastes have widened a little since then!

When I was a child it was hard to imagine a meal without potatoes. Since then, we've embraced pasta and rice enthusiastically and we no longer expect to see potatoes on our plate every day. But they're still one of the most popular vegetables, and no wonder. Potatoes are astonishingly versatile, lending themselves to just about every cooking method, from baking, boiling, steaming, roasting, and frying, to use in breads, pies, cakes, and puddings. And it's good to see that there has been a revival of interest in old-fashioned potato varieties recently, plus the development of some exciting new ones. Gone are the days when the grocer asked, "Reds or whites, love?" Now, in England, we can choose from a range that includes knobbly Pink Fir Apple, yellow-fleshed Yukon Gold, and the mysterious purple-black truffle potatoes. Like all good things, potatoes can be endlessly reinvented while never losing their essential character. Food trends may come and go but I suspect the humble spud will never be out of fashion.

a short history of the potato

Life without the potato is almost unthinkable (no mashed potato, no fries…) but in fact it is a relative newcomer to Europe and North America. Now one of our culinary staples, it very nearly didn't become established at all.

Potatoes have been cultivated in Peru since at least 200 B.C. but it wasn't until the early sixteenth century that Spanish Conquistadors took them to Europe, where they were regarded, along with tomatoes and eggplants, as the work of the devil. They were also believed to be poisonous, which is not so surprising when you consider that they belong to the same family as deadly nightshade.

In 1589, Sir Walter Raleigh introduced the potato to Ireland, when he planted seeds on a 40,000-acre plot near Cork, given to him by Queen Elizabeth I. He neither liked nor understood potatoes though, and eventually ordered them to be uprooted. In France, too, they were unpopular, until Antoine Parmentier convinced Louis XVI that they could

bring an end to famine. He organized court banquets with potatoes in every course, and persuaded Marie Antoinette to wear potato blossoms in her hair and have them embroidered into her evening gowns, thus ensuring that they became fashionable. Meanwhile, in Prussia, Frederick the Great had recognized the potato's potential as a food source and distributed seeds to the peasantry, along with instructions for cultivation and a warning to any who objected that their nose would be cut off if they failed to comply!

Eventually the adaptability of the potato to all types of soils, climates, and cultures made it a staple ingredient throughout the world, particularly in Europe and America. Its crucial role in sustaining entire populations became apparent in 1845, when potato blight hit Europe. This deadly fungus destroyed crops for several years in succession and had an enormous political impact, contributing to general unrest and sowing the seeds of revolution and immigration. Arguably the consequences are still with us today. In Ireland, where the potato had become a major food source, the disaster hit particularly hard. Nearly one and a half million people died, large numbers emigrated, and the country took many years to recover.

In 1995, potatoes became the first vegetable to be grown in space. Today, they remain a major food source, playing a vital role in many cuisines. They are no longer seen as food for the poor; instead, unusual varieties are attractively packaged and sold at a premium price.

The recipes in this book are a tribute to the versatility of potatoes and the affection with which they are regarded throughout the world. If there is a message it is simply this: be adventurous and eat more potatoes!

potatoes are good for us

Contrary to popular belief, potatoes are packed with goodness. They are not fattening, although very often their accompaniments are (butter, cream, cheese, oil …). Plainly cooked potatoes contain only 98 calories per ¼lb. Even when roasting or frying potatoes, it is possible to minimize the amount of fat they absorb by making sure the butter or oil is very hot before adding the potatoes. Here are just some of the health benefits of potatoes:

- They are high in starchy carbohydrate, making them a good source of energy (experts recommend we should increase our intake of starchy carbohydrate foods such as potatoes, bread, pasta, and rice).
- They are high in potassium, which helps to counteract the adverse effects of salt in our diet.
- They contain a useful amount of vitamin C (about 11mg per ¼lb baked potato). The vitamin C content is highest in newly harvested potatoes and decreases during storage and prolonged cooking, or if the potatoes are left to soak in water before cooking.
- They also contain iron and vitamins B1 (thiamin) and B2 (riboflavin).
- They contain no cholesterol and virtually no fat, and are low in sodium.

the most nutritious way to cook potatoes

The most nutritious way to cook potatoes is in their skins, since most of the vitamins and minerals lie in or just beneath the skin. Baking potatoes in their skins, therefore, is an ideal way of preserving all the nutrients. Boiling potatoes in their skins has a dual advantage: not only does it prevent the vitamins leaching out into the cooking water, but it also ensures that the potatoes hold their shape better.

Throughout this book you will notice that some recipes call for the potatoes to be peeled, while in others they are left unpeeled; it is really a matter of personal taste. If you do peel potatoes, peel them as thinly as possible just before cooking. Always boil them in the smallest amount of water, and never leave them in hot water after cooking.

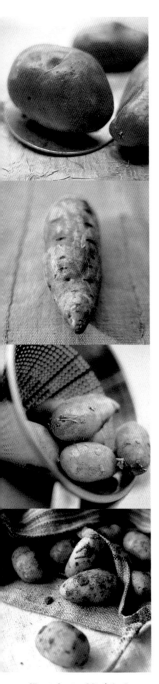

[Top to bottom] Desirée, Sweet, Jersey Royal, Nicola

choosing the right potato

There are some 4,000 varieties of potato available worldwide right now, and even though only a tiny fraction of these appears in the stores there is understandably some confusion about which potatoes are best for which cooking methods.

With just a few exceptions, potatoes can be divided into two main categories:

- Floury potatoes (sometimes called mealy potatoes) are high in starch and have a low water content. This is because the sugar has been converted to starch by the time the potato is harvested. These potatoes become fluffy when cooked, making them suitable for roasting, baking, mashing, and fries. They are not good for boiling, unless you intend to mash them, because they break up.
- Waxy potatoes are low in starch but have a high water content. They usually have a firm texture and a shiny appearance. They keep their shape when cooked, making them suitable for salads or any other occasion when you want to serve them whole. They are also good for sautéing and gratins.

However, this is not the only means of classification. Potatoes can also be categorized according to their age:

- New potatoes (earlies) are traditionally planted early in the year and are available in late spring and early summer. However, modern methods of cultivation mean that "new" potatoes are now imported from other countries throughout the winter – although arguably the flavor of the first homegrown ones is best. Most new potatoes are waxy varieties. When cooking new potatoes, you should add them to boiling salted water rather than putting them in cold water.
- Old potatoes (maincrop) are mainly floury varieties, which have been left in the ground until fully grown and then harvested in the autumn. Unlike new potatoes, they keep well and can be stored for several months in optimum conditions. Old potatoes should be put in cold water and brought to a boil rather than added to boiling water, as this makes them less likely to break up during cooking.

In other countries, such as the US, potatoes are classified by their shape and the color of their skin or flesh – hence recipes calling for red, yellow, russet, or white potatoes.

Below is a guide to the more popular varieties of potatoes and their uses, but let's not forget that whatever the ideal variety for each dish, you can of course choose any potato you like – as long as you bear in mind that the end result will be slightly different. For example, using waxy potatoes instead of floury ones to make mashed potatoes will give a more glutinous texture. Different potato varieties all have their own characteristics and part of the pleasure of cooking with potatoes is experimenting to find out what you like best.

top of the crops

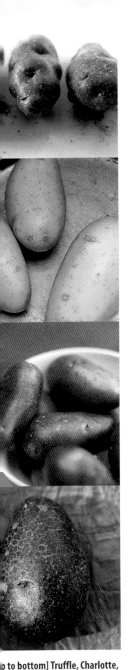

[top to bottom] Truffle, Charlotte, Francine, Shetland Black

Potato varieties	Steaming/ boiling	Salads	Mashing	Roasting	Shallow-frying	Deep-frying	Baking
Atlantic						●	
Bintje	●			●	●	●	
Charlotte	●	●			●		
Chieftan	●						
Desiree			●	●		●	●
Estima	●					●	
Golden Wonder		●	●		●	●	
Jersey Royal	●	●			●		
Kennebec						●	
Kerrs Pink	●		●	●			
King Edward			●	●		●	●
Krantz	●					●	●
Marfona	●						●
Maris Piper			●	●		●	●
Pike						●	
Red Pontiac	●			●			
Red La Soda	●						●
Russet Burbank		●			●	●	
Russet Norkotah							●
Shepody	●					●	●
Truffle	●	●	●	●			
White Rose	●						●
Yukon Gold		●	●			●	●

BUYING AND STORING POTATOES

When choosing potatoes, always look for firm, fresh specimens with a smooth, unblemished skin. Avoid any that are soft and rubbery, that have green or moldy patches, holes, or sprouting eyes. Green patches are caused by exposure to light and indicate that the potato contains an abnormally high level of solanine – a poisonous substance that is not destroyed by cooking. If you discover green patches when peeling your potatoes, the only thing to do is throw them out.

I generally prefer to purchase my potatoes loose from a vegetable market. Pre-washed potatoes are more likely to spoil quickly than unwashed ones, especially when wrapped in plastic. So although the plastic bags of washed potatoes sold by supermarkets seem convenient, they are really only worth buying if you plan to use them within a couple of days. They are also more expensive than loose potatoes. When buying unwashed potatoes, make sure the soil on them is fresh; if it is slimy or smells unpleasant, the potatoes will not be in good condition.

Organic potatoes are readily available now, and are free of the pesticide residues often detected in the skins of conventionally farmed potatoes – making them a better option if you prefer not to peel them. They almost always taste better, too. Conventionally produced varieties have water and nitrogen added, which gives farmers a bigger yield but dilutes the flavor.

New potatoes don't keep for more than a few days. Maincrop varieties, however, can be kept for up to six months if stored correctly. This means in a cool, dark, well-ventilated place, ideally at about 45°F. Below this temperature – for example, in the fridge – the starch will convert to sugar, which spoils the flavor. If you purchase potatoes in a plastic bag, transfer them to a brown paper bag before storing – they will become damp in plastic, causing them to rot.

Surprisingly, potatoes tend to bruise quite easily, so always handle them with care. Bruises will turn black when cooked.

To preserve the nutrients, potatoes should be peeled just before you cook them. However, if you do occasionally need to peel them a few hours in advance, keep them in cold water with a little salt and a slice of white bread to prevent discoloration.

ABOUT THE RECIPES...

- Please note that all recipes serve 4 unless otherwise stated.
- Large eggs and fresh herbs are used unless otherwise stated.

[Top to bottom] Maris Piper, King Edward, La Ratte, French Charlotte

tools of the trade

Although you don't have to buy any special equipment for cooking potatoes, here are a few items I find invaluable. Using them correctly not only gets the job done properly but also saves you time. Always buy the best-quality equipment you can afford.

Deep fryer

You can, of course, deep-fry potatoes in an ordinary pot but deep fryers are safer and cleaner to use. The heat is thermostatically controlled and you can close the lid while the potatoes are frying.

Frying pans

Use these for potato sautés, omelettes, and pancakes. Heavy-duty frying pans, such as cast iron, are best, since they maintain a steady heat level and the food is less likely to burn. Frying pans with ovenproof handles let you transfer food from the stove to the oven to finish cooking.

Grater

You will need a grater for making rösti, boxty, and many other traditional potato dishes that call for grated potatoes. Box graters are easy to use. Otherwise you could use the grating disc on a food processor.

Gratin dishes

These shallow baking dishes have low sides so the food can brown easily in the oven, and a large surface area so you can enjoy the maximum amount of crisp crust. The best ones can be used over direct heat, to let you start off the cooking on the stove before transferring the dish to the oven.

Knives

Good sharp knives are essential for many kitchen tasks. A large, sturdy, cook's knife is best for chopping or slicing potatoes. Sharpen the blade regularly on a steel rod – at least once a week to keep it in prime condition.

Mandoline

A good-quality mandoline with an adjustable blade is an expensive piece of equipment but it is a very efficient way of cutting neat potato slices, as thinly as you like. It can also be used for cutting french fries and matchstick potatoes, and for shredding.

Potato masher

This is the cheapest way of mashing potatoes, although the results won't be quite as smooth as with a potato ricer.

Potato peeler

There are many varieties available but it's best to buy a thin-bladed one. The swivel variety is very good, and also comes in handy for shaving Parmesan cheese. U-shaped peelers, with the blade going straight across the U, can be used with equal ease by right- and left-handers.

Potato ricer or sieve

A potato ricer produces perfect fluffy mashed potato without any lumps at all. A sieve does a pretty good job too, but you will have to push the potato through with a wooden spoon. Buy the largest potato ricer you can find, so you can process the potatoes more speedily.

Don't be tempted to mash potatoes by puréeing them in a food processor, as they will become gluey. Sweet potatoes can be puréed successfully in this way, though.

Roasting pans

Heavy-duty stainless steel or aluminum roasting pans won't buckle in the heat of the oven and can also be used on the stove.

[Top to bottom] French Roseval, Spunta, Red Duke of York, Shetland Black

WHAT COULD BE

more satisfying than a potato soup? Nutritious, warming, and comforting, it can cost next to nothing to prepare (the White Bean and Potato Soup on page 19, for example) or combine the earthy with the extravagant – like my Chilled Potato and Watercress Soup with Caviar Chantilly (page 19). Potato salads, too, vary from the humble to the luxurious. They are staples of cuisines all over the world, whether you choose a spicy Aloo Chat from India (page 42), a Provençal-inspired Grilled Potato and Fennel Niçoise (page 41) or a Moroccan Sweet Potato and Cilantro Salad (page 33). Indeed, for potato salads almost anything goes – the one firm rule is to use boiling potatoes rather than floury potatoes so they keep their shape.

Potatoes might not seem an obvious choice for an appetizer but they don't have to be heavy or filling. It's a question of using them judiciously and combining them with vibrantly flavored ingredients. Potato Fettunta with Gorgonzola Spread and Crumbled Bacon (page 27) make a simple and elegant canapé, while in the Peruvian dish, Causa (page 23), a fiery salsa adds interest to layered purple and saffron potatoes.

SOUPS, APPETIZERS, AND SALADS

potato, smoked bacon, and nettle soup

Heat 1/2 stick of butter in a heavy pot, add the onion and leek, and sweat for 8–10 minutes, until soft. Add the potatoes and cook for 5 minutes. Pour in the stock and bring to a boil, then reduce the heat and simmer for 25–30 minutes. Meanwhile, blanch the nettles in a large pot of boiling water, drain well, and squeeze out the excess water.

Remove half the soup from the pot and blitz to a purée in a blender. Pour it into a clean pot, add the cream, nettles, the remaining soup, nutmeg, and some seasoning, and bring to a boil. Meanwhile, heat the remaining butter in a pan, add the bacon and diced bread, and cook until golden. Pour the soup into bowls, sprinkle the bacon and croûtons on top and serve.

3/4 stick (1/3 cup) sweet butter

1 onion, diced

1 leek, thinly sliced (or, if unavailable, mild onion)

1 1/4 lbs. waxy potatoes, peeled and cut into 1/2-inch cubes

3 cups well-flavored chicken stock

4 ounces (about 2 large handfuls) nettles (or, if unavailable, spinach)

1 1/4 cups light cream

Freshly grated nutmeg

6–8 slices smoked bacon, cut into small dice

2 slices of white bread, crusts removed, cut into 1/2-inch dice

Salt and freshly ground black pepper

tip

NETTLES GROW ALMOST EVERYWHERE IN BRITAIN, so why not use them in this nourishing soup? Pick the tops in spring, when they are young and tender, and wear rubber gloves! Wash them well before using and don't worry – once cooked, they lose their sting.

tattie hushie (potato, cauliflower, and oatmeal soup)

A rich, comforting soup from Lancashire – not Scotland, as the name might suggest.

Heat the butter in a pot, add the leek and cauliflower, and cook gently for a few minutes. Add the potatoes, then cover and sweat for 10 minutes. Mix together the milk and oatmeal and pour them over the vegetables. Add the stock, bring to a boil, and simmer until the vegetables are tender. Blitz the soup to a purée in a blender, then reheat gently and season to taste.

2 tablespoons sweet butter

1 leek, sliced (or, if unavailable, mild onion)

7 ounces cauliflower, cut into small florets (about 4 cups)

1 1/4 lbs. floury potatoes, peeled and diced

2 1/2 cups whole milk

1/2 cup old-fashioned oats

2 1/2 cups well-flavored chicken stock

Salt and freshly ground black pepper

sweet potato, fourme d'ambert, and chipotle chile soup

This lovely soup showcases this delicate vegetable at its best, with a combination of sweet, spicy, and savory flavors.

Cut the chiles in half lengthwise and shake out the seeds. Place the chiles in a bowl, cover with boiling water, and let soak for 30 minutes, then drain and chop. Heat the butter in a pot, add the onion, carrot, celery, and sage, and cook over low heat for 4–5 minutes, until softened. Add the sweet potatoes, potatoes, and chiles, cover, and sweat for 5 minutes. Pour in the chicken stock and bring to a boil, then reduce the heat and simmer for 40–45·minutes, until the vegetables are falling apart. Pour the soup into a blender and blitz until smooth and velvety. Return to the heat and season with nutmeg, salt and, pepper.

Put the cheese and cream in a small pan and heat gently, stirring, until smooth. Pour the soup into serving bowls, pour the cheese cream over the top, and blend in lightly. Scatter the cilantro over the top and serve.

2 chipotle chiles

2 tablespoons sweet butter

1 onion, chopped

1 carrot, chopped

1 celery stalk, chopped

2 sage leaves, chopped

1 lb. white-fleshed sweet potatoes, peeled and chopped

7 ounces potatoes, peeled and chopped (about 1$\frac{1}{3}$ cups)

1 quart well-flavored chicken stock

Freshly grated nutmeg

3 ounces ($\frac{3}{4}$ cup) Fourme d'Ambert cheese (or other mild blue cheese)

$\frac{1}{2}$ cup heavy cream

2 tablespoons chopped cilantro

Salt and freshly ground black pepper

cullen skink (smoked haddock and potato soup)

tip

ALWAYS BUY NATURAL SMOKED HADDOCK, not the lurid, bright-yellow dyed version available from some fish markets, who are concerned more with appearance than with taste.

Cullen skink can be made in various ways and I've probably tried them all in my time. It varies from a broth to a thickened soup, like my recipe below. When I think of smoked haddock I always think of soft poached eggs as an accompaniment, so I decided to add them to this traditional Scottish soup and discovered a real winner.

Put the smoked haddock in a saucepan, pour in the hot milk, and add half the onion and the mace. Bring just to a boil, then add the water. Return to a boil and simmer for 4–5 minutes, until the fish is cooked. Remove from the heat, take out the fish with a slotted spoon, and place in a bowl to cool. Strain the cooking liquid and set aside. Flake the fish, removing the skin and bones.

Melt the butter in a large pot, add the remaining onion, and cook until soft. Add the potatoes and sweat for 5 minutes. Pour in the reserved cooking liquid and simmer until the potatoes are tender. Pour into a blender and blitz to a purée, then pour into a clean pot. Season with nutmeg, salt, and pepper, stir in the flaked fish, and keep warm.

Poach the eggs in the classic manner (see page 104), then remove from the pan and drain well. Pour the soup into soup bowls, place a poached egg in the center of each portion, and sprinkle the parsley over each.

1 lb. natural smoked haddock, on the bone

$2^1/2$ cups hot whole milk

2 onions, sliced

1 blade of mace

$2^1/2$ cups water

$^3/4$ stick ($^1/3$ cup) sweet butter

4 medium-sized floury potatoes, peeled and diced

Freshly grated nutmeg

4 eggs

2 tablespoons chopped parsley

Salt and freshly ground black pepper

Chilled potato and watercress soup with caviar chantilly

CHILLED POTATO AND WATERCRESS SOUP WITH CAVIAR CHANTILLY

Pick the leaves from one bunch of watercress and set aside. Blanch the other bunch and the stalks in boiling water, then drain, refresh in cold water, and drain again. Chop finely.

Heat the butter in a pot, add the onion, leeks, and potatoes, then cover and sweat over low heat until softened. Pour in the chicken stock, add the chopped watercress, and bring to a boil. Simmer for 20–25 minutes, until the potatoes are falling apart. Pour the soup into a blender and blitz to a purée. Let cool, then stir in the heavy cream. Season to taste and chill thoroughly.

Pour into serving bowls, garnish with the reserved watercress leaves, then place a dollop of cream in the center of each portion, and top it with the caviar.

2 bunches of watercress

¹/₂ stick (¹/₄ cup) sweet butter

1 onion, chopped

2 leeks, white part only, chopped

1 lb. floury potatoes, peeled and diced

1 quart chicken stock

¹/₂ cup heavy cream

Salt and freshly ground black pepper

For the caviar chantilly:

¹/₂ cup whipping cream, semi-whipped

2 tablespoons caviar

FAGIOLI BIANCHI ET PATATA (WHITE BEAN AND POTATO SOUP)

Drain the beans, place them in a large pot and cover with fresh water. Add the herbs and bring to a boil, then simmer for 1 hour. Add the potatoes and garlic, and simmer gently for a further 30 minutes, until the beans and potatoes are soft. Pour into a blender and blitz to a smooth purée, then return to the pot, season to taste, and keep warm. If the soup is too thick, thin it with a little water.

Heat half the oil in a frying pan, add the cubes of bread, and fry until golden. Drain on paper towles and sprinkle with the paprika. Pour the soup into serving bowls, sprinkle with the paprika croûtons, drizzle the remaining olive oil over them and serve.

1¹/₂ cups dried cannellini beans, soaked in
   cold water overnight

6 sage leaves

A sprig of rosemary

9 ounces floury potatoes, peeled and cut
   into small dice (about 1³/₄ cups)

4 garlic cloves, crushed

6 tablespoons virgin olive oil

2 slices of thick country bread, cut into
   ¹/₂-inch cubes

1 teaspoon paprika

Salt and freshly ground black pepper

ROasteD sweet potato Bisque with avocaDo anD Lime salsa

Preheat the oven to 400°F. Place the sweet potatoes in a baking pan, pour in ¼ cup of the olive oil and roast for 40 minutes or until tender – don't let them brown too much, though.

Heat the remaining oil in a large pot, add the onion, garlic, and grated ginger, and cook gently for 5 minutes. Add the roasted sweet potatoes, red chile, cinnamon, and some seasoning, then pour in the stock and bring to a boil. Reduce the heat and simmer for 15 minutes. Pour the soup into a blender and blitz to a smooth purée, then pour it into a large bowl. Stir in the cream, maple syrup, and lime juice, and chill thoroughly.

For the salsa, put the avocado cubes in a bowl, add all the remaining ingredients, and mix well. Season to taste.

To serve, pour the soup into chilled soup bowls and place a spoonful of avocado and lime salsa in the center of each one.

1lb. 6oz. (about 4 cups) orange-fleshed
  sweet potatoes, peeled and cut into
  large chunks
6 tablespoons olive oil
1 onion, finely chopped
1 garlic clove, crushed
2-inch piece of fresh ginger root, grated
1 small red chile, seeded and thinly sliced
½ teaspoon ground cinnamon
3 cups good vegetable or chicken stock
½ cup heavy cream
2 tablespoons maple syrup
Juice of 2 limes
Salt and freshly ground black pepper

For the salsa:
1 avocado, peeled, pitted, and cut into small
  cubes
2 plum tomatoes, skinned, seeded, and
  chopped
¼ cup lime juice
2 scallions, chopped
1 small red chile, seeded and chopped
1 tablespoon roughly chopped cilantro
3 tablespoons olive oil

potage parmentier (potato and leek soup)

A well-made soup is both inexpensive and satisfying, and can be served as an appetizer, a light meal, or a main dish. This soup is easy to prepare and forms a base for many different variations (see below). Served chilled, it becomes the classic Vichyssoise.

Heat the butter in a pot, add the onion and leeks, then cover and sweat until tender but not colored. Pour in the stock and bring to a boil. Add the potatoes and simmer for 25–30 minutes, until tender. Pour the soup into a blender and blitz to a very smooth purée. Return to the pot, reheat gently, and stir in the cream and some seasoning. Serve immediately, sprinkled with the chives.

variations

- *Stir in 1½ cups finely chopped herbs with the cream and serve chilled. Tarragon, chervil, and parsley are good.*
- *Blanch 3 or 4 large handfuls of spinach and add along with with the onion and leeks.*
- *Replace the leeks with celery.*

2 tablespoons sweet butter

½ onion, sliced

2 large leeks, white part only, sliced

1 quart well-flavored chicken stock

12 ounces floury potatoes, peeled and chopped (about 2 heaped cups)

½ cup heavy cream

1 tablespoon chopped chives

Salt and freshly ground black pepper

causa

This chilled potato dish from Peru is made differently in every village and town. I particularly like the way it is molded and layered to show off the contrasting colors.

Serves 6–8

Cook the truffle potatoes in a pot of boiling salted water until tender. Drain and leave until cool enough to handle, then peel. Peel the new potatoes and put them in a separate pan along with the saffron. Cover with boiling salted water and simmer until tender, then drain well. Mash the truffle potatoes and new potatoes separately, or push them through a sieve, to give a smooth purée. Beat half the butter into each purée, followed by half the olive oil, and season to taste. Mix the tuna with the mayonnaise and season to taste.

Take 6–8 metal rings, about 4 inches in diameter, and grease the insides with oil. Place a thin layer of truffle potato purée in each one, followed by some of the tuna mixture, then a layer of saffron potato purée, then more tuna. Top with truffle potato again, then tuna, and finish with saffron potatoes. Smooth the tops with a spatula and chill for 2–3 hours, until firm. Meanwhile, mix all the dressing ingredients together, season to taste, and let infuse for 1 hour.

To serve, carefully unmold the potato causa onto serving plates and pour the dressing over and around each one.

12 ounces truffle potatoes (black potatoes)

12 ounces new potatoes (about 3 small to medium ones)

A good pinch of saffron strands

3/4 stick (1/3 cup) sweet butter

1/4 cup olive oil

6 ounces canned tuna in olive oil, drained

1/4 cup good-quality mayonnaise

Salt and freshly ground black pepper

For the dressing:

2 tablespoons vegetable oil

1 garlic clove, crushed

4 scallions, finely chopped

1 habanero chile, seeded and finely chopped

2 plum tomatoes, cut into 1/4-inch dice

2 anchovy fillets, finely chopped

Juice and finely grated zest of 1 lime

1 tablespoon chopped cilantro

1 tablespoon honey

1 teaspoon baby capers, rinsed and drained

A pinch of ground cumin

GRILLED SQUID WITH CHILI-PICKLED POTATOES AND SHALLOTS

Cut the unpeeled potatoes into slices $1/2$-inch thick and place on a tray. Sprinkle with the coarse salt and leave for 1 hour to help extract the liquid. Wash off the salt and dry the potatoes in a cloth. Bring a pot of water to a boil, add the potatoes, and cook for 5 minutes, then drain well.

Put the vinegar, sugar, and chili flakes in a pan and bring slowly to a boil. Pour into a bowl and let cool, then add the potatoes, shallots, garlic, herbs, and $1/4$ cup of the olive oil. Season and let marinate for 30 minutes at room temperature.

Cut each cleaned squid body open to make a flat piece. Using a sharp knife, score the inner side with parallel criss-cross lines about $1/2$-inch apart.

Toss the squid with the remaining olive oil, season, and place scored-side down on a hot ridged grill pan or a barbecue. Cook for 1–2 minutes, then turn and briefly cook the other side. Add to the pickled potatoes while hot, and leave for a further 30 minutes to let the flavors develop. Serve at room temperature with lots of crusty bread.

9 ounces salad potatoes (2–3 small to medium ones)
1 tablespoon coarse salt
$2/3$ cup white wine vinegar
3 tablespoons sugar
$1/2$ teaspoon dried red chili flakes
2 small shallots, sliced into rings
1 garlic clove, crushed
1 teaspoon chopped mint
1 tablespoon chopped cilantro
6 tablespoons olive oil
1 lb. baby squid, cleaned, tentacles set aside
Salt and freshly ground black pepper

patatas tatas

Recently some fellow chefs and I visited Barcelona on a gastronomic tour of the city's famed restaurants. Being typical chefs, we found time between meals to experience some of Spain's legendary tapas bars, serving simple, tasty hors d'oeuvres. Here's a recipe I picked up at one of them.

Cook the potatoes in their skins in boiling salted water until just tender, then drain and cool slightly before peeling them (or leave the skins on if you prefer). Cut into thick slices and set aside.

Heat the butter in a pan, add the onion, garlic, and smoked paprika, and cook gently until softened. Add the tomatoes and cook for 2–3 minutes, until they begin to soften, then season with salt and pepper. Pour in the cream and bring to a boil. Simmer for 2 minutes, then remove from the heat, add the cheese, and stir it in to form a sauce. Place the potatoes in a serving dish, pour the cheese and tomato sauce over them, and serve.

2$^1/_4$ lbs. waxy new potatoes

2 tablespoons sweet butter

1 onion, finely chopped

1 garlic clove, crushed

$^1/_2$ teaspoon smoked paprika

4 plum tomatoes, skinned, seeded, and roughly chopped into large pieces

$^2/_3$ cup heavy cream

5 ounces grated Manchego cheese (1$^1/_4$ cups)

Salt and freshly ground black pepper

cypriot hot potatoes with cracked coriander seeds

Technically not a salad, you may say, but I like to serve it as one. It is full of enticing flavors and aromas, especially when you lift the lid from the pan – try it and you'll see what I mean.

Preheat the oven to 400°F. Heat the olive oil in a flameproof casserole dish or cast-iron pan, add the potatoes, and fry until golden all over. Season lightly, then cover, transfer to the oven and cook for 15–20 minutes, until just tender. Remove the casserole dish from the oven and place over medium heat. Pour in the wine and scatter the cracked coriander seeds on top, then cover with a tight-fitting lid and let steam for 5–8 minutes, until all the liquid has evaporated. Remove the lid, season to taste, and serve.

$^1/_4$ cup olive oil

1 lb. new potatoes (4 small to medium ones), cut in half but not peeled

$^1/_2$ cup dry white wine

2 tablespoons coriander seeds, lightly cracked

Salt and freshly ground black pepper

potato fettunta with gorgonzola spread and crumbled bacon

Fettunta are very similar to crostini or bruschetta – crisp bread croûtes topped with all kinds of ingredients. Here, baked potato slices replace the bread. They make an ideal canapé, appetizer or tidbit.

Preheat the oven to 400°F. Cut each potato lengthwise into slices $1/2$-inch thick (don't peel them) and parboil in salted water for 2–3 minutes. Drain well and dry. Place the potato slices on a baking sheet, brush on both sides with the olive oil, and season with salt and pepper. Bake for 15–20 minutes, until golden.

Meanwhile, grill the bacon until very crisp, then break them up into large pieces and set aside. Put the scallions and gorgonzola in a bowl and crush lightly with a fork to break the cheese down slightly. Stir in the walnut oil and season to taste.

Top the warm potato slices with a good dollop of the gorgonzola mixture. Put the bacon on top and serve.

5 small baking potatoes

$1/4$ cup olive oil

10 strips of bacon

2 scallions, shredded

$4^1/2$ ounces gorgonzola cheese

1 tablespoon walnut oil

Salt and freshly ground black pepper

truffle potato-stuffed quesadillas with crab and chorizo

This makes a great lunchtime dish or an unusual appetizer when you're looking for something a little different.

Boil the truffle potatoes in their skins until tender, then drain well. Peel them and dice roughly. Heat the butter in a pan, add the onion, chile, and garlic, and sweat until softened but not colored. Add the diced potatoes and cook for 12 minutes. Remove from the heat, crush the potatoes coarsely with a fork, and stir in half the cream cheese to bind. Season to taste.

Mix the crab meat with the cilantro, the grated cheese, the diced chorizo, and the remaining cream cheese, and season to taste. Lay out 4 of the tortillas on a flat surface, spread the potato mixture over them, and cover with the crab mixture. Place the remaining tortillas on top and press down lightly. Grill the stuffed quesadillas on a ridged grill pan (or sauté them in a little extra butter in a frying pan) until charred and golden, turning them once during cooking.

To serve, cut the quesadillas into wedges and garnish with sprigs of fresh cilantro. I also like to serve them topped with a dollop of sour cream, grated cheese, and a little hot salsa.

11 ounces truffle potatoes (black potatoes)

2 tablespoon sweet butter

1 onion, finely chopped

1 green chile, seeded and finely chopped

2 garlic cloves, crushed

6 tablespoons cream cheese

9 ounces fresh crab meat (about $1^1/_4$ cups)

2 tablespoons chopped cilantro

$^1/_2$ cup grated mature Cheddar or Monterey Jack cheese

3 ounces chorizo, skinned and cut into $^1/_4$-inch dice

6-inch flour tortillas

Salt and freshly ground black pepper

Sour cream, more grated cheese, and your favorite hot salsa, for serving

Baby beet, potato, and blue cheese salad

Roasting beets in a sweet and sour dressing gives it a wonderful flavor.

Preheat the oven to 400°F. Trim the beets and wash them well. Place in a roasting pan, drizzle with the olive oil and red wine vinegar, then sprinkle with the brown sugar. Roast in the oven for 40–45 minutes, until tender.

Cook the potatoes in their skins in boiling salted water until tender, then drain well and cut in half. Put them in a bowl along with the cooked beets and scatter the cheese on top. Drizzle the walnut oil over them, scatter the walnuts on top, then season with coarse salt and cracked black pepper.

6 baby beets, whole or cut in half, depending on size

3 tablespoons olive oil

1 tablespoon good-quality red wine vinegar

1 heaped teaspoon brown sugar

1 lb. baby new potatoes (about 4 small to medium ones)

1 1/2 cups Stilton or gorgonzola cheese, roughly chopped

3 tablespoons walnut oil

3 tablespoons walnut halves, toasted and roughly chopped

Coarse salt and freshly cracked black pepper

tip

PRESERVED SALTED LEMONS are one of the definitive flavors of Moroccan cooking, used in all types of dishes, from tagines to salads. You can buy them from some delicatessens and large supermarkets.

patatosalata (Cretan potato salad)

Tasty and colorful, this makes ideal summer fare, a reminder of one of the world's loveliest destinations.

Cook the potatoes in their skins in boiling salted water until just tender, then drain and leave until cool enough to handle. Peel the potatoes and place in a bowl.

Make a dressing by whisking together the red wine vinegar, mustard and olive oil. Pour it over the potatoes while they are still warm. Mix in the remaining ingredients and let marinate for at least 3 hours before serving.

1 lb. salad potatoes (about 4 small to medium ones)

1 tablespoon red wine vinegar

1/2 teaspoon Dijon mustard

5 tablespoons olive oil

1 1/4 cups feta or kefalotiri cheese, crumbled into large pieces

1 tablespoon chopped mint

1 teaspoon chopped oregano

1 red onion, thinly sliced

3 scallions, chopped

16 black olives

1 tablespoon finely chopped preserved lemon

Baby beet, potato, and blue cheese salad

warm potato and shellfish salad

This warm shellfish salad is of Spanish origin. The saffron dressing complements the seafood beautifully, vibrant in color and taste.

Heat the olive oil in a large deep pot, add the onion, tomatoes, roasted red pepper, and garlic, and cook over medium heat for 1–2 minutes. Raise the heat to high, add the squid, and cook for 2 minutes, then add the potatoes, fish stock, and sherry, and let cook gently for 20 minutes. Add the clams, mussels, and jumbo shrimp, cover, and cook gently for a further 2–3 minutes. Using a slotted spoon, transfer all the ingredients to a large plate. Strain the juices left in the pot and set aside.

For the dressing, crush the garlic along with the saffron in a mortar. Add the basil and parsley and crush to a paste, then mix in the lemon juice, olive oil, and the reserved cooking juices. Adjust the seasoning to taste and drizzle the dressing over the shellfish. Serve warm, with lots of crusty bread.

tip

TO CLEAN MUSSELS AND CLAMS, scrub them well under cold running water and discard any open ones that don't close when tapped on the work surface. With mussels, you will also need to pull out and discard the "beard".

2 tablespoons olive oil

1 onion, finely chopped

3 plum tomatoes, skinned, seeded, and chopped

1 red pepper, roasted, skinned, seeded, and diced

1 garlic clove, crushed

8 small squid, cleaned and cut into rings

1 lb. small salad potatoes, peeled and diced (about 3 cups)

^{1}/$_2$ cup fish stock

^{1}/$_4$ cup dry sherry

12 ounces clams, cleaned (see Tip)

12 ounces mussels (or, if unavailable, use clams), cleaned (see Tip)

20 raw jumbo shrimp, peeled and de-veined (see Tip on page 139)

For the dressing:

2 garlic cloves, chopped

A good pinch of saffron strands

10 basil leaves

^{1}/$_4$ cup chopped flat-leaf parsley

Juice of 1 lemon

^{1}/$_2$ cup olive oil

Salt and freshly ground black pepper

moroccan sweet potato and cilantro salad

Morocco boasts one of the most exciting cuisines in the world, a subtle blend of African and European influences. On a recent family holiday in Marrakech, I experienced typical street food at the Djema'a al Fna, the world-renowned square where thousands of people gather nightly to enjoy good food and a lively atmosphere. Here's a salad I have adapted from one prepared by a vendor in the square.

Heat $1/2$ cup of the olive oil in a large pot, add the onions, ginger, and chiles, and sauté until tender but not colored. Add the sweet potatoes, saffron, cumin seeds, lemon juice, and smoked paprika, then pour in enough water just to cover. Cover the pot with a lid, reduce the heat, and cook for 10–12 minutes, until the potatoes are just tender. Stir in the cilantro, mint, and preserved lemon, then pour in the remaining oil and adjust the seasoning. Transfer to a bowl and let cool before serving.

$2/3$ cup good-quality olive oil

2 onions, thinly sliced

$1/2$-inch piece of fresh ginger root, finely chopped

2 red chiles, seeded and thinly sliced

1 lb. 5 oz. small, white-fleshed sweet potatoes, peeled and cut into slices $1/8$-inch thick

A pinch of saffron strands

$1/2$ teaspoon cumin seeds, toasted briefly in a dry frying pan

Juice of 1 lemon

$1/2$ teaspoon smoked paprika

3 tablespoons chopped cilantro

1 tablespoon chopped mint

1 tablespoon finely chopped preserved lemon (see Tip on page 30)

Salt and freshly ground black pepper

Roast potato salad with smoked salmon

Roast potato salad with smoked salmon

I have always liked the combination of smoked fish and potatoes. Here, Jersey Royals and a piquant dressing act as the perfect foil for the salmon.

Preheat the oven to 375°F. Wash the potatoes, then put them in a roasting pan, toss with ¼ cup of the olive oil, and season with salt. Roast for about 40 minutes, until golden and tender, then remove from the oven and let cool slightly.

Whisk the vinegar and the remaining olive oil together to make a dressing, and season to taste. Cut the potatoes in half and place in a bowl along with the scallions, capers, gherkins, and chopped eggs. Pour the dressing over them and adjust the seasoning.

Spread the smoked salmon out on 4 serving plates and arrange the potato salad on top. If you're a salmon lover like me, place a little extra salmon on top, too. Sprinkle with the tarragon and serve.

12 ounces (about 3–4) small Jersey Royal potatoes (or, if unavailable, other waxy potatoes)

⅔ cup olive oil

2 tablespoons sherry vinegar

2 scallions, cut into slices ⅛-inch thick

1 tablespoon superfine capers, drained

6 small cocktail gherkins, thinly sliced

2 eggs, hard-boiled and finely chopped

11 ounces thinly sliced smoked salmon

1 teaspoon chopped tarragon

Salt and freshly ground black pepper

Tricolor potato salad

This simple potato salad looks stunning, using three varieties of potatoes that work so well together visually.

Cut the unpeeled potatoes into slices ¼-inch thick, preferably on a mandoline. Cook them separately in pans of boiling salted water for 4–5 minutes, until just tender, then remove with a slotted spoon and place in a bowl.

Make the dressing by whisking the mustard with the vinegar, garlic, and a little salt, then whisking in the oil. Add the herbs, then toss the dressing with the hot potato slices. Adjust the seasoning and serve warm.

7 ounces truffle potatoes (black potatoes)

7 ounces round red potatoes

7 ounces round white potatoes

Salt and freshly ground black pepper

For the dressing:

1 teaspoon Dijon mustard

1 tablespoon red wine vinegar

1 garlic clove, crushed

3 tablespoons virgin olive oil

2 tablespoons each chopped mint and chives

salad monégasque with chargrilled sardines

Salad monégasque is similar to salade niçoise and is prepared daily in cafés and brasseries throughout France. It is normally served on its own but I prefer it with chargrilled fish. Mackerel would work just as well as sardines.

Cook the unpeeled potatoes and the French beans in separate pans of boiling salted water until just tender, then drain well. For the dressing, whisk the vinegar, garlic, mustard, and a little salt together in a large bowl, then whisk in the oil. Add the potatoes and beans to the bowl, then add all the remaining ingredients except the sardines. Toss gently and season with salt and pepper.

Heat a ridged grill pan and brush with a little oil. Place the sardine fillets on the grill and cook for 2–3 minutes on each side, until golden. Arrange the salad on serving plates, top with the chargrilled sardines, and drizzle over them a little of the dressing left in the bowl.

1/2 lb. small new potatoes (about 2 small to medium ones)

5 ounces young green beans (about 1 cup)

4 anchovy fillets, cut into strips

2 teaspoons superfine capers, rinsed and drained

4 radishes, thinly shaved

12 black olives, pitted

1 celery stalk, thinly sliced

12 cherry tomatoes, cut in half

2 hard-boiled eggs, cut into quarters

4 x 8-ounce fresh sardines, filleted

Salt and freshly ground black pepper

For the dressing:

2 tablespoons good-quality white wine vinegar

2 garlic cloves, crushed

1 teaspoon Dijon mustard

6 tablespoons olive oil, plus extra for

salt-baked potato salad

This is an adaptation of an idea by Todd English, renowned chef of Olives Restaurant in Boston. I love the simple idea of filling a baked potato with a salad – I've used a variation of Waldorf salad here, which works wonderfully well with the hot baked potato.

Bake the potatoes until tender (see page 70), then slice a lid off the top of each one. Scoop out a little of the center with a spoon and discard. Combine the salad greens, apples, walnuts, celery, and ham in a salad bowl.

Make the dressing by whisking together the mustard, tarragon, shallots, and vinegar, then gradually whisking in the olive oil until emulsified. Add the vinaigrette to the salad bowl, season, and toss well. Arrange the salad on top of the potatoes, sprinkle the crumbled Roquefort on top, and serve immediately.

4 large floury potatoes

1/2 head Belgian endive, cut into strips

a handful of arugula

2 Granny Smith apples, cored and chopped

2 tablespoons chopped walnuts

1 celery stalk, sliced

3 ounces cooked ham, cut into strips (3/4 cup)

3 ounces Roquefort cheese, crumbled (3/4 cup)

Salt and freshly ground black pepper

For the dressing:

1 teaspoon Dijon mustard

1 tablespoon chopped tarragon

2 shallots, finely chopped

1 tablespoon cider vinegar

1/4 cup olive oil

saffron potato, pear, and fennel salad

Sliced raw fennel has a wonderful aroma and adds a good crunch to potato salads. Serve with grilled fish for a light lunch.

Cook the potatoes in their skins in boiling salted water until just tender, then drain well and leave until cool enough to handle. Peel the potatoes, cut them into slices 1/4-inch thick, and place in a large bowl.

Whisk together all the ingredients for the dressing, pour it over the potatoes, and toss well. Season to taste and leave for about 30 minutes.

Slice the fennel very thinly, preferably on a mandoline (reserve the fronds for garnish), and add to the potatoes. Peel, core, and thinly slice the pear, add to the potatoes, and toss. Adjust the seasoning, garnish, and serve.

12 ounces waxy potatoes, preferably La Ratte or Charlotte

2 fennel bulbs

1 large, ripe Conference pear (or, if unavailable, use a Bosc)

For the dressing:

1/4 cup olive oil

2 tablespoons walnut oil

1 tablespoon sherry vinegar

A good pinch of saffron strands

2 tablespoons honey

Salt and freshly ground black pepper

smoked duck, potato, and cèpe salad

This elegant salad makes a wonderful hors d'oeuvre for a dinner party. Smoked chicken works as well as duck, and is easily available and less expensive.

Cook the potatoes in their skins in boiling salted water until just tender, then drain well. Cut them into slices ¹/₂-inch thick, then fry in the olive oil for 3–4 minutes on each side, until golden. Add the sliced cèpes and the walnuts, and sauté for a minute longer. Season to taste, remove from the heat and keep warm.

For the dressing, combine the shallot, mustard, sherry vinegar, garlic, and herbs in a small bowl, then whisk in both oils and season with salt and pepper. Place the salad greens in a bowl, toss with a little of the dressing, and adjust the seasoning. Arrange the salad greens on 4 serving plates and top with the slices of smoked duck. Scatter the potato mixture on top and drizzle over them the remaining dressing, then serve immediately.

5 ounces new potatoes (2 small to medium ones)
¹/₄ cup olive oil
4 large fresh cèpe (porcini) mushrooms (or chestnut mushrooms), sliced
24 walnut halves
5 ounces mixed salad greens
2 smoked duck breasts, thinly sliced
Salt and freshly ground black pepper

For the dressing:
1 shallot, finely chopped
¹/₂ teaspoon Dijon mustard
2 tablespoons sherry vinegar
1 garlic clove, crushed
1 tablespoon chopped flat-leaf parsley
1 tablespoon chopped tarragon
¹/₄ cup olive oil
2 tablespoons walnut oil

grilled potato and fennel niçoise

A simple but tasty salad, full of the robust flavors of Provence. Don't worry if you haven't got a mortar and pestle for the dressing; use a small blender instead.

Remove any fronds from the fennel and set aside. Peel the fennel with a potato peeler to remove the fibrous outer layer. Cut each bulb in half lengthwise, then cut each half into eighths. Trim off a little of the root from each piece but be careful to leave the layers attached at the root end.

Bring 2 pots of water to a boil. Add the fennel to one and the new potatoes to the other. Cook the fennel for 3–4 minutes, then drain in a colander. Let the new potatoes cook on until they are just tender when pierced with a knife. Drain in a colander and cool slightly before cutting them in half lengthwise. Heat a ridged grill pan, toss the fennel wedges and potatoes in the olive oil, and season with salt and pepper. Cook on the grill, turning them often, until golden and tender.

Meanwhile, prepare the dressing. Place the garlic, basil, and a good pinch of salt in a mortar, and crush to a paste. Stir in the remaining ingredients and season to taste.

Put the grilled potatoes and fennel in a bowl, pour the dressing over them, and garnish with any reserved fennel fronds.

3 fennel bulbs

12 ounces large new potatoes (about 1–2)

1/4 cup olive oil

Salt and freshly ground black pepper

For the dressing:

1 garlic clove, chopped

8 basil leaves

2 red peppers, roasted, skinned, seeded, and finely chopped

10 black olives, pitted and finely chopped

2 shallots, finely chopped

4 anchovy fillets, finely chopped

5 tablespoons olive oil

Juice of 1/2 lemon

aloo chat

tip

TO SHAVE FRESH COCONUT, cut a coconut in half with a saw and pour off the liquid. Knock the base of the coconut hard with a rolling pin to loosen the flesh, then run a knife around the edge – the flesh should come away in one piece. Cut into shavings with a potato peeler or a mandoline.

This Indian salad, served at room temperature, is fantastic with a tart apple and grape chutney. It also makes a nice addition to an Indian meal.

Heat the ghee or clarified butter in a frying pan, add the onion, and cook over low heat until translucent. Add the potatoes, chile, turmeric, ground coriander, cumin seeds, and a little salt, and fry for 10–15 minutes, until the potatoes are lightly browned.

Add the water and bring to a boil. Reduce the heat to a simmer and cook gently until all the liquid has been absorbed and the potatoes are tender. Let cool, then arrange in a serving dish. Scatter the coconut shavings and coriander leaves on top before serving.

1/2 cup ghee or clarified butter (see Tip on page 153)

1 small onion, finely chopped

1 lb. small waxy potatoes, peeled and cut lengthways in half

1 small red chile, seeded and thinly sliced

1 teaspoon ground turmeric

2 teaspoons ground coriander

1 teaspoon cumin seeds, toasted briefly in a dry frying pan

2/3 cup water

Flesh from 1/2 small coconut, cut into shavings (see Tip)

Fresh cilantro leaves, for garnishing

Salt

warm potato salad with ham, shallot, and mustard dressing

The ingredients for this salad form the recipe for the classic French dish jambon persillé (jellied ham with parsley). It occurred to me one day to try a potato salad using virtually the same ingredients. It worked well, so here it is.

Cook the potatoes in boiling salted water until tender, then drain and place in a bowl. Add the ham, shallots, capers, gherkins, and parsley, and toss together.

For the dressing, put the vinegar and mustard in a bowl, whisk in the olive oil, and season to taste. Pour the dressing over the potatoes and toss to blend all the ingredients. Leave for 10–15 minutes to let the potatoes absorb the flavors of the dressing. Serve warm.

1 lb. 6 oz. new potatoes, peeled

4 ounces cooked ham, chopped (about 1 cup)

2 shallots, chopped

2 tablespoons superfine capers, rinsed and drained

8 cocktail gherkins, chopped

3 tablespoons chopped flat-leaf parsley

For the dressing:

1 tablespoon red wine vinegar

1 teaspoon Dijon mustard

1/4 cup olive oil

Salt and freshly ground black pepper

Aloo chat

mashed potato

is the ultimate comfort food, a rich, creamy, soothing purée that seems eternally associated with childhood. Yet recently it's come of age, as chefs have enriched it with more and more butter, cream, and oil, and incorporated new flavors. I've done my share of reinventing it, too, and this chapter contains some of my favorites, such as Charred Onion and Bacon Mash (page 49) and Truffle, Morel and Corn Mash (page 49). But you'll also find recipes here for basic mashed potato (page 46), and traditional dishes such as the Irish Champ (page 50).

Dumplings might not be as popular as mash but they deserve to be. In northern Europe they are something of an art form – delicate and featherlight, an ideal vehicle for soaking up the rich juices of a soup or stew. Potatoes make some of the lightest dumplings of all, like the little Italian gnocchi (see page 51), which are poached and served with a sauce. Like many potato recipes, they lend themselves to an infinite range of variations: you can vary the basic gnocchi recipe by adding different flavorings or, for a complete change, try Sweet Potato Gnocchi with Red Pepper and Basil (page 52).

mash, gnocchi, and dumplings

Everyone knows how to make mashed potatoes but very few people know how to do it properly. For perfect results, follow the tips below:

- Use floury potatoes, such as Yukon Gold or russet Burbank.
- Don't peel the potatoes until just before cooking them, otherwise they will go hard.
- Put the potatoes in a pot of cold water and bring to a boil, rather than putting them straight into boiling water.
- Don't overcook them or they will disintegrate and go mushy.
- Mash them immediately; they will become glutinous if left to stand.
- Work the butter in thoroughly to give a really velvety smoothness.
- Mix in the hot milk gradually; because potatoes vary in starch content, adding too much can make them runny.
- Serve mashed potatoes immediately; they don't reheat well.

perfect mashed potatoes

2 lbs. even-sized floury potatoes, peeled
    and cut into chunks
1 stick ($^1/_2$ cup) sweet butter
$^1/_2$ cup whole milk
$^1/_4$ cup heavy cream
Salt and freshly ground black pepper

Place the potatoes in a pot, cover with cold water, then add a little salt and bring to a boil. Reduce the heat and simmer until tender. Drain well in a colander and return to the pot. Mash with a potato masher or press the potatoes through a potato ricer or sieve.

Beat in the butter with a wooden spoon, then gradually mix in the hot milk, followed by the cream, adding just enough to get the consistency you want. Beat until fluffy and light, then season to taste. The potatoes should be buttery, creamy, and velvety in texture. Now you have the perfect mash!

perfect mashed potatoes

variations on the perfect mashed potato...

parsnip, potato, and honey mustard mash

14 ounces parsnips (about 2 medium), peeled and cut into chunks

9 ounces floury potatoes, peeled and cut into chunks (about 1¹/₂–2 cups)

²/₃ cup whole milk

¹/₂ stick (¹/₄ cup) sweet butter

¹/₄ cup heavy cream

1 tablespoon honey

2 tablespoons whole grain mustard

Salt and freshly ground black pepper

Place the parsnips and potatoes in a pot, cover with cold water, then add a little salt and bring to a boil. Reduce the heat and simmer until almost tender. Drain through a colander and return to the pan.

Pour in the milk and cook for a further 5–8 minutes, until the potatoes are tender.

Remove from the heat, add the butter, cream, honey, and mustard, and mash with a potato masher until smooth. Season to taste.

mashed potatoes with mascarpone and tomatoes

So simple, so tasty. Try it with fish, such as salmon or cod.

3 tablespoons mascarpone cheese, at room temperature

¹/₂ quantity of Perfect Mashed Potatoes (see page 46)

4 scallions, thinly sliced

5 ounces sun-blush tomatoes (see Tip on page 89), cut into small pieces (a scant cup)

Beat the mascarpone cheese into the prepared mash. Carefully stir in the scallions and tomatoes, and serve immediately.

wasabi mashed potatoes

I regularly make horseradish mash, especially as an accompaniment to roast beef for Sunday lunch. It gave me the idea of going one step further and using wasabi – a Japanese horseradish that has a mind-blowing heat. Take great care when adding it to the mashed potatoes. Remember you can add more, but you can't take it away.

This mash is great with all sorts of oriental dishes, as a Fusion alternative to rice or noodles. It's also very good with smoked salmon, believe it or not!

1 lb. 10 oz. floury potatoes, peeled and cut into chunks

¹/₂ stick (¹/₄ cup) sweet butter

¹/₂ cup whole milk

2 teaspoons wasabi (Japanese horseradish)

2 tablespoons chopped chives or scallions

Salt and freshly ground black pepper

Place the potatoes in a pot, cover with cold water, then add a little salt and bring to a boil. Reduce the heat and simmer until tender. Drain well in a colander and return to the pot. Mash with a potato masher or press through a potato ricer or sieve.

Beat in the butter with a wooden spoon, then gradually mix in the hot milk. Add the wasabi and beat until fluffy and light. Season to taste and stir in the chives or scallions.

ratatouille mash with melting olive butter

This dish was created by one of my chefs at the Lanesborough, who inadvertently suggested mixing some ratatouille with creamy mashed potatoes. I tried it and it has become a popular way of serving mash in the hotel. Great with lamb.

¹/4 cup olive oil

1 small onion, finely chopped

3 garlic cloves, crushed

2 ounces eggplant, cut into ¹/2-inch dice (about ¹/2 cup)

¹/4 red pepper, seeded and finely diced

¹/4 yellow pepper, seeded and finely diced

1 small green zucchini, finely diced

1 small golden zucchini or yellow summer squash, finely diced

1 plum tomato, skinned, seeded and finely chopped

¹/2 quantity of Perfect Mashed Potatoes (see page 46)

1 tablespoon chopped basil

¹/2 teaspoon thyme leaves

Salt and freshly ground black pepper

For the olive butter:

¹/2 stick (¹/4 cup) sweet butter

1 tablespoon chopped black olives

1 teaspoon lemon juice

For the olive butter, mix the butter with the olives and lemon juice, and season to taste. Place the butter on a piece of foil and shape it into a cylinder, wrapping it in the foil. Place in the fridge for 2 hours to firm up.

To make the ratatouille, heat the olive oil in a frying pan, add the onion and garlic, and fry until they are just beginning to brown. Add the remaining vegetables and cook over low heat for 8–10 minutes, until softened. Transfer to a bowl, stir in the mashed potatoes and herbs, and season to taste.

Cut the olive butter into slices ¹/4-inch thick and arrange on top of the mash. Serve.

golden mash with bourbon and balsamic drizzle

The American way of serving orange sweet potatoes with sweet spices and whiskey may sound an unlikely combination but in fact it works extremely well. The vinegar helps to cut the sweetness. Serve with grilled or roast chicken.

1 lb. 10 oz. orange-fleshed sweet potatoes

Juice and finely grated zest of ¹/2 lemon

A pinch of freshly grated nutmeg

¹/4 teaspoon ground cinnamon

¹/4 teaspoon ground allspice

3 tablespoons dark soft brown sugar

¹/4 cup balsamic vinegar, plus a little extra for serving

2 tablespoons bourbon

Salt and freshly ground black pepper

Preheat the oven to 400F°. Pierce the potatoes all over with a small, sharp knife, then place on a baking sheet and bake for about 45–50 minutes, until soft. Let cool, then cut in half and scoop out the flesh. Transfer to a food processor, add the lemon zest and juice, spices, and some salt, and blend until smooth.

Combine the sugar, vinegar, and bourbon in a small pan and bring to a boil. Simmer until it forms a light caramel, then add to the potatoes and mix well. Taste, and adjust the seasoning if necessary. Transfer the mash to a serving dish, drizzle over it a little balsamic vinegar, and serve.

CHARRED ONION AND BACON MASH

Perhaps my favorite mash of all. The smoky flavor of charred red onions and crisp bacon combined with velvety smooth mash – it really tastes as good as it sounds!

2 red onions

3 tablespoons olive oil

5 ounces bacon (about 10–12 strips)

1 quantity of Perfect Mashed Potatoes (see page 46)

Salt and freshly ground black pepper

Heat a griddle or a ridged grill pan. Peel the onions and cut them into slices 1/4-inch thick, trying to keep the slices intact. Brush with the olive oil, season with salt and pepper, and grill for 5–8 minutes on each side, until charred and tender. Remove from the grill and leave until cool enough to handle, then cut into small dice. Chargrill the bacon for a few minutes on each side, then chop into small dice also. Add the onion and bacon to the prepared mash and adjust the seasoning. Serve.

CHICKPEA AND OLIVE OIL MASH

3/4 cup chickpeas, soaked in cold water overnight

2 garlic cloves, crushed

1/2 quantity of Perfect Mashed Potatoes (see page 46)

5 tablespoons fruity olive oil

1 tablespoon sesame oil

A pinch of cayenne pepper

Salt and freshly ground black pepper

Drain the chickpeas, then place them in a pot, cover with fresh water, and bring to a boil. Reduce the heat and simmer for 1–1 1/2 hours, until completely tender. Drain, reserving the cooking water. Purée the chickpeas in a blender along with the garlic, a little salt, and enough of the cooking liquid to give a thick, creamy consistency. Add the purée to the hot mashed potatoes, then beat in the olive oil and sesame oil until they have been absorbed. Adjust the seasoning, transfer to a serving dish, and sprinkle the cayenne pepper on top.

TRUFFLE, MOREL, AND CORN MASH

A rather gastronomic mash, made with fresh black truffles and wild mushrooms. It's particularly good with chicken and beef.

1/4 ounce dried morel mushrooms

1 lb. 10 oz. floury potatoes, peeled and cut into chunks

2 ears of corn, husks removed

2/3 cup whole milk

2 tablespoons sweet butter

1/4 ounce fresh black truffle, thinly sliced

1/2 cup heavy cream

2 slices of white bread, crusts removed, cut into strips

Salt and freshly ground black pepper

Soak the dried mushrooms in 1/2 cup hot water for 1 hour, then drain and chop roughly. Set aside.

Place the potatoes in a pot, cover with cold water, then add a little salt and bring to a boil. Reduce the heat and simmer until tender. Meanwhile, using a small, sharp knife, shuck the kernels from the cobs. Place in a pot, cover with the milk, and bring to a boil. Reduce the heat and simmer for 10–12 minutes,

until the corn is tender, then place in a blender and blitz to a smooth purée.

Drain the potatoes in a colander and return to the pot. Mash with a potato masher or press through a potato ricer or sieve. Stir the corn purée into the hot mash.

Heat half the butter in a frying pan, add the morels and truffle slices, and sauté for 1–2 minutes. Season to taste and mix into the mash. Fold in the cream and adjust the seasoning. Finally, fry the bread strips in the remaining butter until golden. Put the mash in a serving bowl and top with the fried bread.

champ

According to Irish folklore, this Northern Irish dish should always be made with buttermilk. It is sometimes referred to as stelk or cally.

Put the potatoes in a large pot, cover with cold water, then add a little salt and bring to a boil. Reduce the heat and simmer until just tender. Drain in a colander, return to a low heat, and let dry out for 2 minutes.

In a separate pan, heat the buttermilk or milk, cream, and half the butter. Add the scallions and cook gently for 5 minutes to remove the raw flavor.

Mash the potatoes until smooth, then, with a wooden spoon, beat in the buttermilk and onion mixture a little at a time to give a light, fluffy consistency. Season to taste, place in a serving dish, and make a well in the center. Add the remaining butter and serve immediately, as the butter slides temptingly down the silky potatoes. Watch your guests dive in, in an effort to get a little of that melting butter and soft, fluffy mash.

$2^1/_4$ lbs. floury potatoes, peeled and cut into
   chunks
a scant cup buttermilk or whole milk
$^1/_2$ cup heavy cream
$^3/_4$ stick ($^1/_3$ cup) sweet butter, cut into
   small pieces
A bunch of scallions, chopped
Salt and freshly ground black pepper

basic potato gnocchi

Here's the Lanesborough's basic recipe for gnocchi, or little potato dumplings, a staple of Italian cuisine. They're very versatile. Try adding mixed herbs, finely chopped cooked mushrooms, or other flavorings to the dough.

Serve gnocchi with melted butter, tomato sauce, or another sauce of your choice.

900g (2lb) floury potatoes, peeled and cut into chunks
275g (10oz) plain flour
1 egg
Freshly grated nutmeg
Salt and freshly ground black pepper

Place the potatoes in a pot, cover with cold water, add some salt, and bring to a boil. Reduce the heat and simmer until tender, then drain well and dry in a clean lint-free towel. Press the potatoes through a fine sieve into a large bowl.

Sift in the flour, then add the egg, and season with nutmeg, salt, and pepper. Mix well and turn out onto a lightly floured work surface. Knead for 2–3 minutes to form a smooth, slightly elastic dough. With floured hands, roll the dough into long cylinders, ³/4 inch in diameter, then cut into ³/4-inch lengths. Roll each one lightly over the tines of a fork so it is grooved all over. Place on a floured baking tray until ready to cook.

Bring a large pot of water to a boil, reduce the heat so it is simmering, and add the gnocchi in batches, being careful not to crowd the pot. Poach for 3–4 minutes, until the gnocchi rise to the surface. Remove with a slotted spoon, drain well, and keep warm in a dish while you cook the rest.

sweet potato gnocchi with red pepper and basil

For the red pepper sauce, heat the olive oil and butter in a pan, add the onion and garlic, and cook over low heat for 3–4 minutes, until softened. Pour in the wine and bring to a boil, then add the chopped peppers and tomato paste and cook for 5–8 minutes. Pour in the stock and return to a boil. Add the herbs and simmer for 20 minutes. Pour the sauce into a blender and blitz until smooth, then season with salt and pepper.

For the gnocchi, preheat the oven to 400°F. Place the sweet potatoes on a baking tray and bake until tender. Cut them in half, and scoop out the flesh with a spoon. Blitz in a food processor or press through a sieve to obtain a smooth purée. Place in a bowl, add the egg, flour, three-quarters of the Parmesan, and some salt and pepper, and mix together thoroughly to form a smooth, fairly firm dough. Shape into classical, Italian gnocchi (see page 51) or simple round balls.

Cook the gnocchi in batches in a large pot of simmering water for 5–8 minutes, until cooked through (cut one open to check), then remove with a slotted spoon and arrange in an ovenproof dish. Put the butter in a pan with 3 tablespoons of water and bring to a boil so the butter melts. Add the chopped basil and simmer for 1 minute, then pour this mixture over the gnocchi. Sprinkle the remaining Parmesan on top and place in an oven preheated to 400°F for 5 minutes, until the cheese is bubbling and golden. Reheat the pepper sauce and pour onto 4 plates. Top with the gnocchi and serve.

1 lb. 6oz. orange-fleshed sweet potatoes

1 egg

1¹/₂ cups all-purpose flour

4 ounces Parmesan cheese, freshly grated (2 cups)

³/₄ stick (¹/₃ cup) sweet butter

A good bunch of basil, chopped

Salt and freshly ground black pepper

For the red pepper sauce:

1 tablespoon olive oil

2 tablespoons sweet butter

1 small onion, chopped

1 garlic clove, crushed

5 tablespoons dry white wine

2 large red peppers, seeded and chopped

1 tablespoon tomato paste

²/₃ cup chicken or vegetable stock

A few basil stalks

A sprig of thyme

potato and pumpkin dumplings with horseradish

German-style Knödel such as these are a typical northern European way of making the best of potatoes. They can be served simply with melted butter but I also like to serve them as a garnish for a rich beef and vegetable stew.

Heat half the butter in a frying pan, add the pumpkin cubes, and fry until golden all over. Season with salt and pepper and add the water. Reduce the heat, cover the pan, and cook until the pumpkin is tender. Let cool.

Place the potatoes in a pot, cover with cold water, then add a little salt and bring to a boil. Reduce the heat and simmer until tender, then drain well and mash until smooth. Add the egg yolks, cornstarch, semolina, half the flour, and the horseradish. Season with nutmeg, salt, and pepper, and mix well.

Using your hands, shape the mixture into dumplings the size of golf balls, pressing a cube of pumpkin into the center of each one. Spread the remaining flour over a baking tray or plate, and roll the dumplings in it until they are evenly coated.

Put the dumplings in a large, wide pot of boiling salted water, reduce the heat, and simmer for 15–20 minutes, until cooked through (cut one open to check). Meanwhile, melt the remaining butter. Remove the dumplings from the pot with a slotted spoon and place in a serving dish. Pour the melted butter over them and serve.

1 stick (^{1}/2 cup) sweet butter

5 ounces peeled pumpkin, cut into ^{1}/2-inch cubes (about ^{3}/4 cup)

^{1}/2 cup water

3 lbs. floury potatoes, peeled and cut into chunks

3 egg yolks, lightly beaten

3 tablespoons cornstarch

3 tablespoons semolina

^{3}/4 cup all-purpose flour

2 tablespoons freshly grated horseradish

Freshly grated nutmeg

Salt and freshly ground black pepper

POTATO, LEMON, AND RICOTTA PANSOTI WITH SALSA DI NOCI

*Pansoti are a speciality of Liguria in Italy. The name means "little tummies"
– a quirky description of their shape – and classically they are stuffed with
an herb filling. My potato, lemon, and ricotta filling is equally delicious.*

Bake the potatoes until tender (see page 70). Leave until cool enough
to handle, then cut them in half, scoop out the flesh into a bowl, and
crush with a fork. Mix in the ricotta, milk, parsley, lemon zest, and
cinnamon, season with nutmeg, salt, and pepper, and let cool.

For the pasta dough, place the flour in a large bowl and make a well in
the center. Mix together the wine, water, and egg, and pour into the
well. Carefully fold the flour into the center and mix thoroughly to
form a dough. Turn out and knead for 4–5 minutes, then set aside to
rest for 10–15 minutes. Roll out the dough through the stages of a
pasta machine, taking it to the narrowest setting, and cut into 3-inch
triangles. Place a little of the potato filling in the center of each triangle,
brush the edges of the dough with a little water, and fold the triangle
in half, pressing down firmly to seal.

For the salsa, simmer the walnuts in boiling water for 4–5 minutes,
then drain well and peel off the thin brown skin. Put the walnuts,
breadcrumbs, and Parmesan in a blender, add the ricotta cheese and
pine nuts and blend until smooth. Mix in the milk and olive oil, and
season to taste. Poach the pansoti in a large pot of boiling salted water
for about 3–4 minutes, until tender, then drain. Place in a serving dish
and pour the walnut sauce over them. Sprinkle the Parmesan cheese
on top and pour melted butter around them.

2¼ lbs. red-skinned potatoes

a heaped ½ cup ricotta cheese

2 tablespoons milk

2 tablespoons chopped flat-leaf parsley

Zest of 1 lemon, finely grated

¼ teaspoon ground cinnamon

Freshly grated nutmeg

2 tablespoons freshly grated Parmesan
cheese

2 tablespoons butter, melted

Salt and freshly ground black pepper

For the pasta dough:

3½ cups all-purpose flour

3 tablespoons dry white wine

1 tablespoon water

1 egg

For the salsa di noci:

1 cup walnut halves

½ cup fresh white breadcrumbs (about
2 slices)

1½ cups freshly grated Parmesan cheese

½ cup ricotta cheese

a scant ½ cup pine nuts

¼ cup whole milk

¼ cup extra virgin olive oil

potato noodles with shrimp in their own sauce

Preheat the oven to 400°F. Wrap each potato in foil (this makes them softer and easier to peel) and bake until tender, then remove from the foil and peel. Press the potato flesh through a sieve or a potato ricer into a large bowl. Mix in the Parmesan, flour, and some salt and pepper. Make a well in the center, pour in the eggs, and bring together to form a dough. Knead the dough for 1–2 minutes, then wrap in plasticwrap and let rest for 30 minutes.

Shape the dough into a long roll about 1 inch in diameter and cut it into slices about 1/2-inch thick. Shape them into noodles by rolling each one under the palm of your hand on a floured surface until it is a torpedo shape about 2 inches long. Place on a floured baking tray and set aside.

For the shrimp, heat the olive oil in a large pan, add the reserved heads and shells from the shrimp and sauté over high heat for a couple of minutes. Add the chopped vegetables and cook for 4–5 minutes, until softened. Pour in the brandy and wine, and boil for 5 minutes, then stir in the tomato paste and cook for a further 5 minutes. Pour in enough water to cover the shells, bring to a boil, then reduce the heat, add the cream, and simmer for 10–12 minutes, until the mixture has thickened enough to coat the back of a spoon. Pulverize briefly in a blender or food processor, then strain through a fine sieve, or wire-mesh strainer, into a clean pan. Add the shrimp and poach them for 2 minutes in the sauce, until cooked through. Whisk in the chilled butter, a few pieces at a time, and season to taste. Keep warm.

Poach the potato noodles in a large pot of boiling salted water for 2–3 minutes; they are ready when they rise to the surface. Remove with a slotted spoon, toss with the melted butter, and season to taste. Arrange on serving plates and pour the prawns in their own sauce over them. Scatter chervil leaves on top and serve.

14 ounces floury potatoes

1 cup freshly grated Parmesan cheese

1¼ cups all-purpose flour

2 eggs, lightly beaten

½ stick (¼ cup) sweet butter, melted

Salt and freshly ground black pepper

Chervil leaves, for garnishing

For the shrimp:

¼ cup olive oil

20 raw tiger shrimp, peeled and de-veined (see Tip on page 139) – set aside the heads and shells

1 heaped cup finely chopped mixed carrot, leek, and onion

2 tablespoons brandy

100ml (3½ fl oz) dry white wine

1 tablespoon tomato paste

⅔ cup heavy cream

2 tablespoons chilled sweet butter, cut into small pieces

THIS CHAPTER includes some favorite

potato basics, such as baked and roast potatoes, as well as a wide range of gratins. The best-known gratin, of course, is the dauphinois (page 60). This dish always provokes controversy but if you bake sliced potatoes slowly in lots of cream you are bound to end up with something delicious whether it's "authentic" or not. A lovely variation on this is Janssons Frestelse (page 67), a Swedish dish that includes anchovies and onions. The important thing to remember about gratins is to use the right sort of dish – it should be shallow enough to allow the top to brown evenly.

The humble baked potato deserves a more interesting treatment, occasionally, than the standard pat of butter and sprinkling of grated cheese. It makes a wonderful container for all sorts of flavors – a couple of my favorites are Smoked Cheddar "Rarebit" Soufflé (page 72) and Cretan Feta, Olive, Toasted Pine Nuts and Oregano (page 71), but the possibilities are endless.

Plain roast potatoes (page 76) are so delicious with the Sunday roast that it's tempting just to leave it at that, but if you fancy a change you will find plenty of other ideas in this chapter to inspire you.

gratins,
bakes, and
roasts

Le vrai dauphinois

What makes an authentic gratin dauphinois? It has been a source of debate for years, so perhaps it should come down to individual preference. One thing is agreed, though. On no account should it include cheese – or does that start another dispute?

Preheat the oven to 375°F. Peel the potatoes, wipe them dry, and slice them thinly lengthwise on a mandoline. Take a large, flameproof, earthenware dish, rub it lightly with the garlic, and then sprinkle with salt. Grease the dish liberally with some of the butter, and arrange overlapping slices of potato in it, seasoning between each layer.

Mix the eggs with the cream and milk, and pour this mixture over the potatoes to cover them. Dot with the remaining butter. Start cooking the potatoes on top of the stove until the liquid comes to a boil, then place in the oven and cook for 1–1^1/4 hours, until the potatoes are tender, almost all the liquid has been absorbed, and a rich golden crust has formed on the surface. Serve direct from the dish, while very hot.

2^1/4 lbs. waxy potatoes

2 garlic cloves, crushed

1 stick plus 1 tablespoon (^{1}/2 cup plus 1 tablespoon) sweet butter

2 eggs, beaten

1^1/4 cups heavy cream

1^3/4 cups whole milk

Salt and freshly ground black pepper

Crisp crushed potato with goat cheese, chives, and thyme

Preheat the oven to 400°F. Cook the potatoes in their skins in boiling salted water until just tender, then drain and leave until cool enough to handle. Peel the potatoes, put them in a bowl, and crush lightly with a fork. Mix in the grated goat cheese, milk, butter, and herbs, and season with salt and pepper.

Whip the cream lightly, and fold it through the potato mixture. Transfer to a buttered gratin dish and bake for 12–15 minutes, until a golden crust has formed. Serve hot from the oven.

1 lb. new potatoes (about 4 small to medium ones)

1 crottin de Chavignol goat cheese, coarsely grated

5 tablespoons goat milk

^{1}/2 stick (^{1}/4 cup) sweet butter

1 tablespoon chopped chives

1 teaspoon thyme leaves

^{1}/2 cup heavy cream

Coarse salt and freshly ground black pepper

BRANDADE OF HALIBUT WITH CRAB GRATIN

Brandade is usually prepared with salt cod but here I have used halibut. What I particularly like about this dish is the crab crust, which makes a lovely crisp topping for the creamed halibut.

Put the milk, cream, garlic, thyme, bay leaf, and some salt in a pot and bring to a boil. Reduce the heat to a simmer, add the halibut fillet, and poach for 10–12 minutes. Remove the fish with a slotted spoon and place in a large bowl. Add the potatoes to the cooking liquid and simmer until tender. Remove with a slotted spoon, place in another bowl, and mash to a purée. Remove the skin from the halibut and add the fish to the mashed potato. Beat in the olive oil and enough of the cooking liquid to form a smooth, creamy brandade. Adjust the seasoning and stir in the chopped chives.

Preheat the oven to 400°F. Butter four 4- to 5-inch metal rings, place them on a baking tray, and fill with the brandade. Level off the top with a spatula. Mix together the breadcrumbs, crabmeat, and softened butter, and sprinkle on top of the brandade. Drizzle a little olive oil over them and bake for 12–15 minutes. Meanwhile, prepare a light sauce: put the fish stock in a pan and bring to a boil, then whisk in the butter, a few pieces at a time. Add the basil, and season to taste.

Place the brandades on serving plates, remove the rings, and pour the sauce around each. Garnish with basil and serve.

2¹/2 cups whole milk

2 cups heavy cream

4 garlic cloves, crushed

2 sprigs of thyme

1 bay leaf

1 lb. 6 oz. halibut fillet, skin on

1 lb. 2 oz. floury potatoes (about 4 medium ones), peeled and chopped

6 tablespoons olive oil, plus a little extra for drizzling

1/4 cup chopped chives

a heaped 1/3 cup fresh white breadcrumbs

7 ounces fresh white crabmeat (about 1 cup)

2 tablespoons sweet butter, softened

Coarse salt and freshly ground black pepper

For the sauce:

2/3 cup fish stock

1/2 stick (1/4 cup) sweet butter, cut into small pieces

10 basil leaves, torn, plus extra for garnishing

Red Potato, Onion, and Herb Cheese "Brik"

Briks are a staple of Moroccan cooking, deep-fried turnovers of thin, phyllo-like pastry stuffed with various fillings such as egg, tuna, and vegetables. In this recipe, the briks are made using potato slices to replace the pastry. Is this heresy or creativity?

Place the potato slices in a bowl and season with salt and pepper. Melt three-quarters of the butter and pour it over the potatoes while it is still hot. Let them soften for about 30 minutes. Meanwhile, carefully mix the diced cheese with the herbs and whipped cream, and place in the fridge.

Gently heat the oil in a pan, add the onions, and cook for 4–5 minutes, until softened. Add the sugar and cook for 5 minutes, until the onions are caramelized. Remove from the pan and let cool.

Heat the remaining butter in a pot, add the Swiss chard, and cook for 4–5 minutes, until tender and wilted. Season with salt and pepper.

Preheat the oven to 375°F. To assemble the briks, heat 4 blini pans or tartlet molds, 4- to 5-inches in diameter (heating them seals the potato and helps prevent it sticking). Drain excess butter from the softened potatoes, and arrange overlapping potato slices inside each mold, letting them overhang the edges. Spread the Swiss chard over the bottom, top with the creamed herb cheese mixture, and finally with the caramelized onion. Carefully fold over the overlapping potato to cover the filling. Press down lightly and place on a baking sheet. Bake for 25–30 minutes, until the potatoes are golden, cooked through, and crisp. Cool slightly, then tip out onto serving plates and keep them warm.

For the sauce, boil the stock and cream together until reduced in volume by a third. Add the herbs, season to taste, and pour around the briks.

3 large russet Burbank potatoes, peeled and cut lengthwise into slices $1/8$-inch thick

1 stick ($1/2$ cup) sweet butter

7 ounces Neufchâtel cheese, cut into $1/2$-inch dice

2 tablespoons chopped mixed herbs, such as chives, basil, parsley, chervil, and tarragon

6 tablespoons heavy cream, lightly whipped

2 tablespoons olive oil

2 red onions, thinly sliced

1 tablespoon brown sugar

5 ounces Swiss chard (or spinach), leaves only (about 2 large handfuls)

Salt and freshly ground black pepper

For the sauce:
$2/3$ cup cup chicken stock

$1/2$ cup heavy cream

1 tablespoon chopped mixed herbs

Red potato "brik", cooling before being tipped out, and awaiting its rich herb sauce

GRATIN of NEW potatoes AND JERUSALEM ARTICHOKES WITH mustard AND Lemon

It's a great pity that Jerusalem artichokes are not as popular as they deserve to be. I love these tuberous little gems, which look like potatoes and can be used in much the same way – deep-fried, boiled, or baked, for example. Here they combine wonderfully well with the potatoes in this creamy, mustard-flavored gratin.

Preheat the oven to 350°F. Cook the new potatoes and Jerusalem artichokes in separate pots of boiling salted water for 8–10 minutes, until just tender, then drain in a colander. When they are cool enough to handle, peel the potatoes.

Heat the oil in a frying pan, add the onion, garlic, and parsley, and cook over low heat until tender. Add the cream, mustard, and lemon zest, and bring to a boil, then season with nutmeg, salt, and pepper.

Cut any large potatoes and artichokes in half, leaving smaller ones whole. Place them in a buttered gratin dish, pour over them the mustard sauce, sprinkle on the Gruyère and bake for 30 minutes, until golden and bubbling.

1 lb. very small new potatoes (about 5–7)

7 ounces Jerusalem artichokes, peeled

2 tablespoons olive oil

1/2 onion, finely chopped

1 garlic clove, crushed

2 tablespoons chopped parsley

11/2 cups heavy cream

1 tablespoon whole grain mustard

Zest of 1 lemon, finely grated

Freshly grated nutmeg

2 ounces Gruyère or Swiss cheese, grated
  (1/2 cup)

Salt and freshly ground black pepper

sweet potato and eggplant Lasagne

Here's a meatless lasagne that contains no pasta, replacing it with thinly sliced sweet potatoes instead.

Place the sweet potato slices on an oiled baking sheet and bake for 10–12 minutes, until just soft. Let cool. Toss the eggplant slices with the olive oil and garlic, and place on a baking sheet. Season, and bake for 20 minutes, until just soft, then let cool.

For the tomato sauce, heat the oil in a pan, add the onion and garlic, and fry until softened. Add the white wine and bring to a boil, then add the tomatoes and bay leaf and simmer for 20 minutes. Season to taste.

For the basil sauce, melt the butter in a pan, stir in the flour, and cook gently, stirring, for a few minutes. Gradually stir in the milk, then bring to a boil and simmer gently for a few minutes, until thickened. Season to taste and stir in the basil.

In a bowl, mix together the ricotta, cream, eggs, and Parmesan, and season to taste.

Preheat the oven to 375°F. To assemble the lasagne, spread a third of the tomato sauce over the bottom of a 10- to 12-inch square earthenware dish, cover with half the sweet potato slices, and season well. Add another layer of tomato sauce, followed by half the eggplant. Sprinkle half the grated Cheddar on top. Pour the ricotta mixture over this and spread evenly, then top with the remaining sweet potato. Spread over them the rest of the tomato sauce, and top with the remaining eggplant. Pour the basil sauce on top. Sprinkle on the last of the Cheddar and bake for 15–20 minutes, until golden and bubbling.

3 white-fleshed sweet potatoes, peeled and cut on the diagonal into slices $^{1}/_{4}$-inch thick

3 large eggplants, cut on the diagonal into slices $^{1}/_{2}$-inch thick

$^{1}/_{4}$ cup olive oil

1 garlic clove, crushed

1 heaped cup ricotta cheese

3 tablespoons heavy cream

2 eggs, beaten

$^{1}/_{2}$ cup freshly grated Parmesan cheese

1 cup grated Cheddar cheese

Salt and freshly ground black pepper

For the tomato sauce:

1 tablespoon olive oil

1 onion, finely chopped

1 garlic clove, crushed

2 tablespoons white wine

2 x 14-ounce cans of tomatoes, chopped

1 bay leaf

For the basil sauce:

2 tablespoons sweet butter

$^{1}/_{4}$ cup all-purpose flour

$2^{1}/_{2}$ cups whole milk

3 tablespoons chopped basil

janssons frestelse (jansson's temptation)

Legend has it that this Swedish dish tempted a religious fanatic to break his vow to renounce earthly pleasures – hence the name. Whatever the truth, it's certainly delicious.

Preheat the oven to 375°F. Generously butter a gratin dish. Heat the butter in a pan, add the onions, garlic, and anchovies, and sweat for 8–10 minutes, until tender but not colored. Layer the potatoes and onion mixture in the gratin dish, adding a grinding of pepper to each layer as you go. Mix the cream and milk together and pour them over the potatoes, which should be completely covered. Cover the dish with foil and bake for 45 minutes. Remove the foil, sprinkle the breadcrumbs on top, and return to the oven until bubbling and golden. Serve straight from the oven.

2 tablespoons sweet butter, plus extra for greasing the dish

2 onions, thinly sliced

2 garlic cloves, crushed

6 anchovy fillets, chopped

1 lb. 10oz. waxy potatoes, peeled and thinly sliced

2$^{1}/_{2}$ cups heavy cream

$^{2}/_{3}$ cup whole milk

1$^{3}/_{4}$ cups fresh white breadcrumbs (about 3 slices)

Freshly ground black pepper

potato and cheese-stuffed chillies rellenos

Preheat the oven to 400°F. Cut a slit in the end of each poblano chile to let the steam be released during cooking. Brush the chiles with a little oil and roast in the oven for 5–10 minutes, until the skins are lightly charred and blistered. Place in a plastic bag and seal it. Let them steam for 5 minutes, then, using a small knife, carefully peel off the skin. Slit each chile open from top to bottom, and remove the seeds.

Cook the potatoes in boiling salted water until just tender, then drain and place in a bowl. Crush with a fork, mix in the goat cheese, and season to taste. Stuff the chiles with this mixture and arrange them in a single layer in a baking dish.

For the sauce, heat the oil in a frying pan, add the red chiles, garlic, and scallions and cook for a couple of minutes, until softened. Add the tomatoes, corn tortillas, brown sugar, and oregano, and cook over gentle heat for 10 minutes. Pour into a blender and blitz to an almost smooth but still slightly textured sauce. Pour the sauce over the stuffed chiles and bake for 10–15 minutes. Scatter with the grated Cheddar, pour the sour cream over that, and serve.

8 poblano chiles

Vegetable oil, for brushing

12 ounces new potatoes (about 3 small to medium ones), peeled

1¹/4 cups crumbled firm goat cheese

³/4 cup grated Cheddar cheese

¹/4 cup sour cream

Salt and freshly ground black pepper

For the sauce:

¹/4 cup vegetable oil

2 red chiles, seeded and chopped

2 garlic cloves, crushed

4 scallions, chopped

14-ounce can of tomatoes, chopped

4 corn tortillas, chopped

2 tablespoons brown sugar

1 tablespoon chopped oregano

Potato and cheese-stuffed chiles rellenos, before sauce has been poured on top, prior to baking

tHe uLtimate
BakeD potato

4 large, floury potatoes

¹/4 cup coarse sea salt or Kosher salt

¹/2 stick (¹/4 cup) sweet butter

Freshly cracked black pepper and sea salt

Preheat the oven to 400°F. Using a small brush, scrub the potatoes thoroughly under running water to remove any dirt. Pat them dry, then prick the skins all over with a small knife. Scatter the coarse salt into a baking pan and place the potatoes on top. Bake for 1–1¹/4 hours, depending on size, until tender.

Remove the potatoes from the oven, cut a cross in the top of each one, and squeeze the potato gently to open it out. Top with the butter, cracked black pepper, and sea salt.

baked potato fillings

Leek, mustard, and parsley

4 large, floury potatoes

3 tablespoons olive oil

1 large leek, finely chopped

2 tablespoons grain mustard

1 cup grated strong Cheddar cheese

1/4 cup heavy cream

2 tablespoons sweet butter

3 tablespoons chopped flat-leaf parsley

Salt and freshly ground black pepper

Bake the potatoes until tender (see page 70), then cut a lid off each one. Carefully scoop out the flesh, leaving a thin shell, and put it into a bowl.

Heat the olive oil in a pan, add the leek and cook over low heat for 8–10 minutes, until tender. Add the leek to the potato flesh along with the mustard, Cheddar, and cream, and mix well. Finally mix in the butter and parsley. Season to taste, then return the mixture to the potato shells and reheat in the oven for a few minutes before serving.

Cretan feta, olive, toasted pine nuts, and oregano

4 large, floury potatoes

1/2 stick (1/4 cup) sweet butter

1/4 cup olive oil

1 cup Greek feta cheese, cut into 1/4-inch cubes

2 tablespoons currants, soaked in hot water for 30 minutes and then drained

2 tablespoons pine nuts, toasted

6 green olives, pitted and chopped

2 tablespoons chopped oregano

Salt and freshly ground black pepper

Bake the potatoes until tender (see page 70), then cut a lid off each one. Carefully scoop out the flesh into a bowl, add the butter and oil, and mash lightly. Gently fold in the remaining ingredients. Fill the potato shells with the mixture and return to the oven for 5–6 minutes to heat through before serving.

mozzarella, basil, and sun-blush tomatoes

4 large, floury potatoes

8 garlic cloves

2 tablespoons olive oil

4 good handfuls of basil leaves, roughly chopped

4 onces sun-blush tomatoes, cut into small pieces (about 2/3 cup)

9 ounces buffalo mozzarella, cut into 1/4-inch dice (about 1 1/4 cups)

Salt and freshly ground black pepper

Bake the potatoes until tender (see page 70). Meanwhile, place the unpeeled garlic cloves in a baking pan, pour the oil over them, and roast in the oven for 25–30 minutes, until golden and caramelized. Remove the skins and mash the flesh coarsely in a bowl. Add the basil, mozzarella, and tomatoes, and season lightly.

Make an incision or a cross in the center of each potato and open it up. Fill with the cheese and tomato mixture, and return to the oven for 8–10 minutes, until the mozzarella is bubbling.

baked potato fillings

dolcelatte, scallions, and chives

4 large, floury potatoes

**5 ounces dolcelatte (or gorgonzola)
   cheese (about 1¼ cups)**

¼ cup heavy cream

½ stick (¼ cup) sweet butter

2 egg yolks

1 tablespoon chopped chives

6 scallions, shredded

Salt and freshly ground black pepper

Bake the potatoes until tender
(see page 70), then cut a lid off
each one. Carefully scoop out
the flesh into a bowl and mash
while hot. Add the dolcelatte,
cream, and butter, and blend
well. Mix in the egg yolks, chives,
scallions, and some seasoning,
then fill the potato shells with
the mixture. Return to the oven
until golden.

asparagus, wild mushroom, romano and baked eggs

4 large, floury potatoes

½ stick (¼ cup) sweet butter

6 medium asparagus spears

2 tablespoons olive oil

**3 ounces trompette de la mort (black
   chanterelle) mushrooms (or other wild
   mushrooms), cut into large dice**

4 eggs

¼ cup heavy cream

1½ cups grated Romano cheese

Salt and freshly ground black pepper

Bake the potatoes until tender
(see page 70), then cut a lid off
each one. Carefully scoop out
the flesh into a bowl and mash
lightly with the butter.

  Blanch the asparagus in
boiling water for 3 minutes, then
drain well and chop. Heat the
olive oil in a pan, add the
asparagus and mushrooms, and
sauté over medium heat for 2–3
minutes. Add to the potatoes
and season to taste. Fill the
potato shells with the mixture,
and then press it down with the
back of a spoon to create a

hollow in the center of each one.
  Crack an egg into each hollow,
pour over it a tablespoon of
cream, and sprinkle with the
grated Romano. Season with salt
and pepper. Replace the lids and
return the potatoes to the oven
for 10–12 minutes, until the eggs
have just set.

smoked cheddar "rarebit" soufflé

4 large, floury potatoes

2 tablespoons sweet butter

1¼ cup all-purpose flour

⅔ cup whole milk

¼ cup beer

1 teaspoon English mustard

2 drops of Worcestershire sauce

a heaped cup of Cheddar cheese

3 eggs, separated

1 tablespoon chopped chives

Salt and freshly ground black pepper

Bake the potatoes until tender
(see page 70), then cut a lid off
each one. Carefully scoop out
the flesh into a bowl and mash
until smooth.

  Melt the butter in a pan, add
the flour, and cook for 1 minute.

Gradually stir in the milk and bring to a boil to make a thick sauce. Add the beer, mustard, and Worcestershire sauce, then stir in the grated cheese and cook very gently for 2–3 minutes, until it has melted. Season with salt and pepper. Stir this sauce into the mashed potato, then add the egg yolks and adjust the seasoning. Whisk the egg whites until stiff, then gently fold them into the potato mixture with a metal spoon.

Carefully fill the potato shells with the soufflé mixture. Return to the oven and bake for 25 minutes, until golden and risen. Garnish with chopped chives and serve.

SOUR CREAM, SMOKED MACKEREL, AND HORSERADISH

4 large, floury potatoes

2 egg yolks

¹/₄ cup sour cream

2 tablespoons creamed horseradish

5 ounces smoked mackerel fillet, skinned

A small handful of arugula leaves, roughly chopped

Salt and freshly ground black pepper

Bake the potatoes until tender (see page 70), then cut a lid off each one. Carefully scoop out the flesh into a bowl and mash until smooth. Beat in the egg yolks, sour cream and horseradish. Flake the smoked mackerel into pieces and mix with the potato, then add the arugula leaves and season with salt and pepper. Fill the potato shells with the mixture and return to the oven for 5–6 minutes, until golden.

MINI BAKED POTATOES WITH SOUR CREAM AND CAVIAR

A simple yet extravagant pre-drinks appetizer. It's also good served with grilled fish.

24 small new potatoes

2 tablespoons chopped chives

¹/₂ cup sour cream

¹/₄ ounce Sevruga caviar

Bake the potatoes until tender (see page 70) – they will take 20–30 minutes, depending on size. Then, with a small knife, make a cross in the top of each potato and use your thumbs and forefingers to squeeze it gently open. Mix together the chives and sour cream and spoon a dollop onto each potato. Top with the caviar and serve immediately.

moroccan baked potato skins

Here's a tasty snack with a spicy touch, although it's not really authentically Moroccan – I like to sprinkle some grated Cheddar over the potato skins during the final few minutes of cooking.

Preheat the oven to 425°F. Cut the skin off the potatoes so it is about 3/4-inch thick, wash it thoroughly, and dry well. Place in a large baking dish.

Mix together all the remaining ingredients except the cheese, pour them over the skins, and toss well together. Place in the oven and bake for about 35 minutes, until golden and crisp. Sprinkle the Cheddar cheese on top and return to the oven until melted and bubbling.

1 lb. 6 oz. large floury potatoes

1/2 cup olive oil

1 tablespoon good-quality harissa paste

1/2 teaspoon ground cumin

1/2 teaspoon ground coriander

1/2 teaspoon ground cinnamon

1/4 teaspoon turmeric

2 garlic cloves, crushed

3/4 cup grated Cheddar cheese

Salt and freshly ground black pepper

the definitive roast potato

As with all simple things, it's worth taking the trouble to get these right. Here are a few tips to help you make perfect roast potatoes:

- Floury potatoes such as russet Burbank (also known as "russet" and "Idaho") produce a fluffy interior, while waxy varieties give a smoother texture. I prefer to use floury potatoes but both are good.
- Peel the potatoes just before cooking them; don't leave them soaking in water.
- Parboiling the potatoes before roasting breaks down their structure, which means that the cooking time is reduced and the outside becomes crisper.
- Make sure the oil in the roasting pan is very hot (almost smoking) before adding the potatoes but let allow it burn. If the oil isn't hot enough, the potatoes will be greasy.
- For really crisp potatoes, make sure they are completely dry before adding them to the hot oil.
- Don't turn the potatoes until they are golden on one side.
- Season the potatoes only when they are cooked; otherwise the salt will make them mushy.
- Serve roast potatoes as soon as they are ready, so they don't lose their crispness.
- I like to cook roast potatoes alongside the meat so they absorb some of the flavor. However, the meat juices can make them slightly soggy. If you like really crisp potatoes, roast them in a separate pan.

roast potatoes

1 lb. 10 oz. floury potatoes, peeled and cut
   into large, even-sized pieces
¹/₄ cup vegetable oil (or fat from the roast)
Salt and freshly ground black pepper

Preheat the oven to 400°F. Place the potatoes in a large pot, cover with cold water, then add a pinch of salt and bring to a boil. Reduce the heat and simmer for 10–15 minutes, until almost tender. Drain in a colander and leave for 5 minutes to dry.

Heat the oil in a large roasting pan until very hot. Add the potatoes to the hot oil and turn them to coat them evenly. Roast in the oven for 30–40 minutes, until golden and crisp, turning them halfway through. Season with salt and pepper and then serve.

tip

TO PREPARE YOUR OWN FRAGRANT GARLIC SALT, separate the cloves of 1 head of garlic, peel them, and slice thinly on a mandoline. Spread the garlic out on a non-stick baking sheet and bake in an oven preheated to 200°F for 3–4 hours, until withered and dry. Let cool, then place in a food processor or blender along with 4 ounces coarse sea salt or Kosher salt (about ¹/₂ cup) and blitz for 30 seconds to combine. Do not overprocess or the salt will be too fine. Stored in an airtight container, this should keep indefinitely.

variations

- *Add 1 tablespoon dried or fresh herbs to the potatoes before placing them in the oven.*
- *Add a favorite spice, such as Cajun seasoning, paprika, or garlic salt (see Tip, above).*

roast potatoes with herbes de provence

Generally I am not keen on using dried herbs but when roasting potatoes like this, I make an exception to the rule. These potatoes are very good served with lamb cutlets that have been marinated for about an hour in a mixture of olive oil, crushed garlic, rosemary, and orange zest, then grilled.

12 medium baking potatoes

¼ cup olive oil

1 teaspoon dried herbes de Provence

Coarse salt and freshly ground black pepper

Preheat the oven to 425°F. Cut the unpeeled potatoes in half lengthwise, then score the flesh-side of each half in a criss-cross fashion. Arrange on a baking tray, cut-side up. Pour the olive oil over them, season with salt and pepper, and sprinkle the dried herbs on top. Roast in the oven for 45–50 minutes, until tender, golden and crisp.

roast red-skinned potatoes with chile and horseradish crème fraîche

Preheat the oven to 400°F. Place the whole, unpeeled potatoes in a large roasting pan, pour the olive oil over them and toss well. Season with salt and pepper and tuck in the fresh thyme. Roast for 35–40 minutes, until tender and golden, then let cool slightly. Meanwhile, mix together the horseradish, crème fraîche, chile, and chives, and season to taste. Cut the potatoes in half, arrange on a serving plate, and top with the chile and horseradish crème fraîche.

1 lb. 2 oz. baby red potatoes

¼ cup olive oil

8 sprigs of thyme

2 tablespoons freshly grated horseradish root

½ cup crème fraîche (or, if unavailable, heavy cream, or mixture of ¾ heavy cream to ¼ sour cream)

1 large red chile, seeded and chopped

2 tablespoons chopped chives

Salt and freshly ground black pepper

Roast sweet potatoes with cardamom, chile, and cinnamon

Preheat the oven to 400°F. In a bowl, toss the sweet potatoes along with the cracked cardamom, cloves, cinnamon stick, and bay leaves. Heat the oil and half the butter in an ovenproof frying pan, add the sweet potatoes and spices, and toss in the hot fat for 5 minutes. Transfer to the oven and roast for 30–35 minutes, until the potatoes are tender and golden.

Remove the spices from the potatoes, add the remaining butter, the chile sauce, and some salt, and toss well.

1 lb. 5 oz. orange-fleshed sweet potatoes, peeled and cut into ¹/₂-inch dice

6 black cardamom pods, cracked (see Tip)

3 cloves

1 cinnamon stick

2 small bay leaves

2 tablespoons vegetable oil

¹/₂ stick (¹/₄ cup) sweet butter

2 tablespoons hot chile sauce

Salt

tip

ALTHOUGH YOU CAN BUY READY-GROUND CARDAMOM it tends to lose its flavor very quickly. I've found the best and quickest way to grind your own is to place whole pods in a blender or food processor and blitz for 30 seconds. Transfer to a fine strainer and sift the ground seeds through, leaving the pods behind.

Roast tikka masala potatoes

Preheat the oven to 400°F. Cook the potatoes in a pot of boiling salted water for 5–8 minutes, until they are just tender but still with a bite. Drain them in a colander.

Melt the ghee or clarified butter in a flameproof roasting pan on the stovetop, add the mustard seeds, and fry until they begin to pop. Add the coriander seeds, cardamom pods, nigella seeds, ginger, chile, curry leaves, and turmeric, and cook for 2 minutes. Add the potatoes and stir to coat them in the spices. Add the water and stir again. Place in the oven and roast for 20–25 minutes, until the potatoes are golden and crusty with the spices. Season to taste and serve immediately.

1 lb. 5 oz. small waxy potatoes, whole or cut in half, depending on size, and peeled

¹/₃ cup ghee or clarified butter (see Tip on page 153)

¹/₂ teaspoon black mustard seeds

1 teaspoon coriander seeds, toasted briefly in a dry frying pan

8 black cardamom pods, cracked (see Tip)

¹/₄ teaspoon nigella seeds (black onion seeds)

1-inch piece of fresh ginger root, finely chopped

1 green chile, seeded and thinly sliced

6 fresh curry leaves

A pinch of turmeric

¹/₂ cup water

Salt and freshly ground black pepper

Roast tikka masala potatoes straight from the oven

BaY-STUDDED POTATOES WITH ROSEMARY AND OLIVE OIL

Preheat the oven to 400°F. With a small knife, cut each potato across its width in slices about ¹/2-inch thick, stopping ¹/2-inch before the bottom so the slices are still joined at the base. Season with salt and pepper and insert a few bay leaves in the cuts in each potato. Place the potatoes in a roasting pan, pour the oil over them, and brush with a little of the melted butter. Roast in the oven for 30–40 minutes, until tender.

Brush with the remaining butter, scatter the rosemary over the top, and return to the oven for 10–15 minutes, until golden. Drain and sprinkle with coarse salt.

variation

Add 4 ounces pancetta, cut into lardons, and some whole peeled garlic cloves to the roasting pan before pouring the oil over them.

8 large new potatoes

16 bay leaves

3 tablespoons olive oil

³/4 stick (¹/3 cup) sweet butter, melted

4 sprigs of rosemary

Coarse salt and freshly ground black pepper

WHO CAN RESIST fried potatoes, in

any shape or form? Crisp, succulent, and unbelievably
moreish, they might have been designed expressly to tempt
us from healthy eating resolutions. In fact, they aren't
necessarily as high in fat as you might think. As long as the
cooking oil is the correct temperature, the potatoes should
be sealed quickly and won't absorb too much of it. Deep-
fried potatoes should always be drained well on paper towles
before serving, to avoid greasiness.

This chapter explains how to make perfect sautéed
potatoes and fries, with several variations on the theme.
Sautéed potatoes can be a sophisticated accompaniment to
grilled meat and fish, but I think they come into their own as
simple breakfast or brunch dishes, such as Bubble and
Squeak (page 86), Sauté Potatoes with Tomato Tapenade and
Fried Egg (page 85) or a new twist on hash browns (page 88).

Like so many potato dishes, fritters and potato cakes
make an ideal vehicle for other flavors. They work particularly
well with Indian spices – try the Aloo Tikki (page 98) – but
also have a real affinity with Mediterranean ingredients.

sautés,
fritters, potato
cakes, and fries

sauté potatoes

1 lb. 6 oz. medium-sized waxy new
  potatoes
¼ cup vegetable oil
2 tablespoons sweet butter
1 tablespoon chopped parsley (optional)
Salt and freshly ground black pepper

Cook the whole, unpeeled potatoes in boiling salted water until almost tender. Drain in a colander and leave until cool enough to handle, then carefully peel off the skins. Cut the potatoes into slices roughly ½-inch thick.

Heat the oil in a large frying pan, add the potatoes, and fry quickly to develop the color; avoid turning or tossing them until they are crisp and browned underneath. Add the butter and, when it is foaming gently, toss it with the potatoes until they become beautifully golden in color. Season with salt and pepper, then place in a serving dish and sprinkle with chopped parsley, if you like.

classic Lyonnaise potatoes

Sauté 1 thinly sliced onion in butter until golden and caramelized, then stir it into the sautéed potatoes before adding the seasoning. Lyonnaise potatoes used to be made with puréed onion, but now sautéed onion is the norm.

sauté potatoes with juniper berries, rosemary, and emmenthal

1 teaspoon juniper berries
1 quantity of Sauté Potatoes (see left)
1 tablespoon chopped rosemary
⅓ cup Emmenthal cheese, cut into ¼-inch
  cubes
Salt and freshly ground black pepper

Put the juniper berries in a mortar and crush to a fine powder. Make the sautéed potatoes in the usual way but after adding the butter, season them with the juniper, along with salt and pepper. Sprinkle the rosemary and cheese over them, toss together quickly, and transfer to a serving dish.

IRRESISTIBLE sauté potatoes

patatas catalan

1 red pepper, cut in half and seeded

¹/4 cup olive oil

3 ounces chorizo or merguez sausage, roughly chopped

1 garlic clove, crushed

12 black olives

1 quantity of Sauté Potatoes (see page 84)

1 tablespoon chopped parsley

Salt and freshly ground black pepper

Preheat the oven to 400°F. Place the pepper halves on a baking sheet, coat with half the olive oil, and roast for 20–25 minutes, until blistered and blackened. Let cool, then peel off the skin and cut the pepper into long strips.

Heat the remaining oil in a frying pan, add the sausage and garlic, and fry for 1 minute, until the sausage is crisp and golden. Add the red pepper and olives and toss together. Add the sautéed potatoes, toss, and adjust the seasoning. Garnish with parsley.

sauté potatoes with crisp artichokes and wilted arugula

3 small globe artichokes

¹/4 cup olive oil

a large handful of arugula leaves

6 basil leaves

1 quantity of Sauté Potatoes (see page 84)

Salt and freshly ground black pepper

Break the stalks off the artichokes, then slice off the tops. Pull off and discard the tough, dark outer leaves. Cut the artichokes in half to expose the choke (hairy fibers). Quickly scrape out the choke, then cut the artichokes into slices ¹/2-inch thick.

Heat the oil in a large frying pan, add the artichokes and cook for 2 minutes. Add the arugula and basil leaves and cook for 1 minute, until wilted, then mix in the sautéed potatoes. Adjust the seasoning and serve.

sauté potatoes with tomato tapenade and fried egg

Everybody loves fried eggs and potatoes. In this recipe, I go one step further and top them with a piquant tomato relish. I also use the relish as a dip for bread, and get regular requests for it from guests.

2 tablespoons olive oil

4 farm fresh eggs

1 quantity of Sauté Potatoes (see page 84)

1 cup Parmesan cheese shavings

For the tomato tapenade:

2 ounces sun-dried tomatoes (about ¹/3 cup)

2 tablespoons baby capers

7–8 green olives, pitted

1 large garlic clove, crushed

1 teaspoon chopped rosemary

¹/2 teaspoon lemon juice

2 tablespoons olive oil

For the tapenade, put all the ingredients in a blender or small food processor and blitz to a coarse purée, then set aside.

Heat the oil in a frying pan and fry the eggs. Spoon the tapenade onto the sautéed potatoes, arrange the eggs on top, and garnish with Parmesan shavings. Serve.

tip

THE TOMATO TAPENADE KEEPS WELL in the fridge and in fact is better when left for a day or two so the flavors can infuse.

Quail eggs make a nice change from hen's eggs, cooked in the same way.

BUBBLE AND SQUEAK

Until recently bubble and squeak was only cooked at home, an ideal way of using up leftover potatoes, but now it regularly appears on British restaurant menus. Its name supposedly comes from the noise the ingredients make in the pan. The cabbage can be replaced with other ingredients, such as Brussels sprouts and spinach. The addition of a little crisp bacon, although not traditional, is very good.

Heat the oil and butter in a large frying pan, add the onion and garlic, and sauté until tender. Add the cabbage, season well, and toss with the onion and garlic. Now add the cooked potatoes and crush with a fork. Toss together until lightly browned, then season to taste and serve.

2 tablespoons olive oil

3 tablespoons sweet butter

1 onion, finely chopped

2 garlic cloves, crushed

4 ounces cooked savoy cabbage, roughly chopped (about 2 cups)

1 lb. boiled potatoes, (about 4 small to medium ones) peeled

Salt and freshly ground black pepper

TIP

ALWAYS USE YOUR OWN FRESH WHITE BREADCRUMBS rather than buying the commercial variety that look and taste like sawdust. To make your own, simply place the bread (crusts removed) in a food processor or blender and blitz to a fine texture – simple as that!

POTATO CUBES WITH CRISPY BACON AND HERB GREMOLATA

Place the potatoes in a pot, cover with cold water, then add a little salt and bring to a boil. Reduce the heat and simmer until the potatoes are almost but not quite cooked. Drain in a colander and cool slightly.

Mix together the herbs, lemon zest, and breadcrumbs, and season with salt and pepper. Season the potatoes, then dip them in the beaten egg whites, and coat in the herb crumbs.

Heat a dry frying pan, add the bacon, and fry for 2–3 minutes, until golden and crisp. Remove with a slotted spoon and keep warm. Add the oil to the pan, followed by the potatoes, and fry until golden all over. Return the bacon to the pan, toss with the potatoes, and serve.

1 lb. 6 oz. small baking potatoes, peeled and cut into $1/2$-inch cubes (about $4^1/2$–5 cups)

$1/4$ cup chopped mixed herbs, such as tarragon, parsley, and chives

Zest of $1/2$ lemon, finely grated

4 ounces fresh white breadcrumbs (about $2^1/2$ cups)

2 egg whites, lightly beaten

10-12 strips smoked bacon, chopped into small pieces

3 tablespoons vegetable oil

Salt and freshly ground black pepper

Potato cubes with crispy bacon and herb gremolata

CYPRIOT HASH BROWNS WITH HALOUMI IN PITA BREAD

Hash browns are crisp fried potatoes. Outside America they tend to be made with grated cooked potato. Americans, however, prefer more rustic diced potatoes. In this recipe I use them as part of a great sandwich with Cypriot cheese.

Put the unpeeled potatoes in a pot, cover with cold water, add a little salt, and bring to a boil. Reduce the heat and simmer until tender, then drain and let cool. Peel the potatoes and cut them into $1/2$-inch dice. Place in a bowl, add the onion, oregano, garlic. and olives, then season with salt and pepper.

Whisk together all the ingredients for the dressing and season to taste.

Heat half the oil in a large frying pan until very hot, add the potato mixture, and fry until the potatoes are crisp, tossing them as you cook; they should be brown and crusty all over. Remove from the heat and keep warm.

Heat a ridged grill pan until smoking. Dip the haloumi slices in the remaining oil, season, and then chargrill for 1–2 minutes, until golden and lightly charred on both sides.

Grill the pita breads until warm, then split them open. Fill with the hash brown mix, then lay the slices of grilled haloumi on top. Drizzle the dressing over that, close the lid, cut in half, and enjoy!

1 lb. floury potatoes

1 red onion, chopped

1 tablespoon chopped oregano

1 garlic clove, crushed

10 black olives, pitted and chopped

6 tablespoons olive oil

12 slices of haloumi cheese

4 pita breads

Salt and freshly ground black pepper

For the dressing:

$1/4$ cup olive oil

Juice of 1 lemon

1 tablespoon superfine capers, rinsed and drained

2 tablespoons sherry vinegar

1 tablespoon chopped chives

tortilla basquaise

Heat the oil in an 8-inch omelette pan, add the potatoes, and fry for 2–3 minutes, until sealed on both sides. Add the onion and cook until both onion and potato are golden. Season with salt and pepper and add the chorizo. Cover with a lid and cook over low heat for 20 minutes or until tender, stirring occasionally.

Beat the eggs with the saffron water and a little seasoning. Pour them over the potato mixture and spread out evenly. Cook over low heat, uncovered, for 8–10 minutes, until just set (if necessary, put the pan under a hot broiler for a minute or two to set the top). Gently run a spatula around the edge of the tortilla to loosen the edges, then invert the tortilla onto a plate. Let cool before cutting into wedges. Serve with a crisp green salad.

1/4 cup good-quality olive oil

14 ounces russet Burbank potatoes, peeled and thinly sliced (about 2 1/2–3 cups)

1 onion, thinly sliced

3 ounces chorizo, skinned and thinly sliced

5 large eggs

A pinch of saffron strands, soaked in 2 tablespoons hot water

Salt and freshly ground black pepper

caramelized potatoes with tomato, thyme, and marjoram

I have always had rather a sweet tooth so this potato dish hits the right note in my estimation. It makes the most of the flavors of southern France, the sweet sun-blush tomatoes working particularly well with the garlic and highly perfumed marjoram. Try serving these potatoes as an accompaniment to a plain roast leg of lamb.

Scrub the potatoes well under cold running water, then dry thoroughly on a kitchen towel. Heat the olive oil in a large, heavy frying pan, add the potatoes, and cook over medium heat for 15–20 minutes, until lightly browned all over and almost tender. Reduce the heat and add the butter, herbs, garlic, chile, and tomatoes. Cook for 3–4 minutes, tossing the potatoes continually. Finally, sprinkle the sugar over them and cook for 1–2 minutes longer, until the potatoes are caramelized. Adjust the seasoning and serve.

2 1/4 lbs. small new potatoes

6 tablespoons olive oil

1/2 stick (1/4 cup) sweet butter

3 sprigs of thyme

3 sprigs of marjoram

3 garlic cloves, crushed

1 small red chile, seeded and finely chopped

4 ounces sun-blush tomatoes, chopped (about 2/3 cup)

2 teaspoons caster sugar

Salt and freshly ground black pepper

tip

SUN-BLUSH TOMATOES are sweet, semi-dried tomatoes marinated in oil and herbs. You should be able to find them in delis and some supermarkets.

pan-fried potato and fruit terrine

This unusual terrine goes particularly well with slices of baked ham or with game. It's best made a day or two before you need it. Not only does this enhance the flavor but it also makes it easier to slice before frying.

I first published this recipe in The Complete Masterchefs *(Weidenfeld & Nicolson) two years ago. Since then I have streamlined it slightly and just couldn't leave it out of this collection of potato recipes.*

Serves 8–10

Preheat the oven to 350°F. Stretch the bacon by running the back of a knife along each one, then use them to line a 2-pound loaf pan or terrine dish, overlapping them slightly and letting them overhang the top of the pan.

Heat the olive oil in a frying pan, add the onion, and sauté until golden. Transfer to a plate and let cool. Peel the potatoes and grate them coarsely. Put them in a lint-free towel and squeeze out excess liquid, then put them into a large bowl. Add the onion, dried fruit, eggs, cream, potato flour, and finally the cheese. Mix well and season with nutmeg, salt, and pepper. Pack the mixture into the bacon-lined loaf pan and fold the overlapping bacon over the top. Cover with a piece of lightly greased foil, place in the oven, and cook for about $1^{1}/_{2}$ hours, until soft when tested with a skewer. Let cool, then place in the fridge to set firm.

To serve, turn the terrine out and cut it into slices $^3/_4$-inch thick. Fry in the butter until golden and slightly crisp.

1 lb. bacon

$^1/_4$ cup olive oil

1 onion, finely chopped

$1^1/_2$ lbs. waxy potatoes

$^3/_4$ cup mixed dried fruit, such as prunes, apples, and apricots, cut into $^3/_4$-inch dice

3 eggs

$^1/_2$ cup heavy cream

2 tablespoons potato flour (or arrowroot)

5 ounces Beaufort or Gruyère cheese, cut into $^1/_2$-inch cubes

Freshly grated nutmeg

2 tablespoons sweet butter

Salt and freshly ground black pepper

CRISPY potato and goat cheese ricotta fritters

tip

THESE FRITTERS ARE PARTICULARLY GOOD served with a tart tomato or apple chutney and garnished with arugula leaves.

Light, feathery, and cheesy – potato fritters that everyone will love. I like to serve these as a vegetarian hors d'oeuvre. If you can't find goat cheese ricotta, ordinary ricotta will be fine.

Put the potatoes in a pot, cover with water, add a little salt, and bring to a boil. Reduce the heat and simmer until tender, then drain well in a colander. Return the potatoes to the pot and dry them out over a low heat. Mash with 1 tablespoon of the butter until smooth, and then beat in the egg yolks. Keep warm.

Dice the remaining butter and put it in a pan along with the water and a little salt. Bring to a boil so the butter melts, then gently rain in the flour and beat with a spatula until the mixture is smooth and leaves the sides of the pan clean. Reduce the heat to a minimum, and cook for 1 minute, beating constantly. Remove from the heat and let cool slightly, then beat in the eggs one at a time. Mix in the mashed potato mixture and then add the ricotta. Beat well together and season to taste.

Heat some oil to 325°F in a deep-fat fryer or a large, deep pot. Take some of the potato mixture in an oiled soupspoon, drop it into the hot oil, and fry a few at a time for 3–4 minutes, until puffed up and golden. Remove with a slotted spoon and drain on paper towles. Sprinkle with salt and serve.

1 lb. floury potatoes, peeled and cut into chunks (about 1¹/2 cups)

3 tablespoons sweet butter

2 egg yolks

¹/2 cup water

¹/2 cup all-purpose flour, sifted

2 eggs

5 ounces goat cheese ricotta (about 1¹/4 cups)

Oil, for deep-frying

Salt and freshly ground black pepper

spicy potato fritters

These Indian-style potato fritters are made with sliced white sweet potatoes dipped in a delicate spicy batter and fried until crisp. The kachumber salad makes an ideal accompaniment.

Put the flour, garam masala, mustard seeds, turmeric, cumin seeds, and baking powder in a bowl and mix well. Stir in enough iced water to make a thick batter, then add the chiles, scallions, and cilantro. Let rest for 20 minutes.

For the salad, mix the tomatoes, red onion, chile, garlic, oil, and lemon juice in a dish, and season to taste. Arrange on a serving plate, scatter the chopped cilantro on top and let stand at room temperature for 30 minutes.

Heat the oil to 350°F in a deep-fat fryer or a deep pot. Dip the potato slices in the batter and fry in batches for about 3–4 minutes, until golden, turning them as they cook. Remove with a slotted spoon and drain on paper towles. Serve hot with the kachumber salad.

1¼ cups besan gram flour

1 tablespoon garam masala

¹/₂ teaspoon black mustard seeds

¹/₂ teaspoon turmeric

1 teaspoon cumin seeds, toasted briefly in a
    dry frying pan and then crushed

¹/₂ teaspoon baking powder

Iced water, to mix

2 green jalapeño chiles, seeded and finely
    chopped

3 scallions, finely chopped

1 tablespoon chopped cilantro

Vegetable oil, for deep-frying

3 white-fleshed sweet potatoes, peeled and
    cut into slices ¹/₈-inch thick

For the kachumber salad:

2 beefsteak tomatoes, sliced

1 small red onion, thinly sliced

1 green jalapeño chile, seeded and finely
    chopped

1 garlic clove, crushed

1 tablespoon plus 1 teaspoon peanut oil or
    olive oil

Juice of ¹/₂ lemon

1 tablespoon chopped cilantro

Salt and freshly ground black pepper

potato kibbeh with Lamb, feta, and mint

Kibbeh is a Middle Eastern dish traditionally made of finely ground meat mixed with onion, spices, and cracked wheat. There are lots of variations throughout the Middle East – for example, the Egyptians prefer to replace the wheat with ground rice. Here's a potato version of kibbeh with a meat filling, plus a couple more variations on the theme.

Place the cracked wheat in a bowl, add the boiling water, and leave for 20–25 minutes, until the water has been absorbed and the wheat is swollen and fluffy. Let cool, then mix with the mashed potato, egg, melted butter, spices, and some salt and pepper. Place in the fridge while preparing the filling.

Heat the olive oil in a frying pan until smoking hot. Season the lamb, and fry in the hot oil with the ground allspice for 10–15 minutes, until cooked through. Transfer to a bowl. Heat the butter in the same pan, add the onion and pine nuts and cook until golden. Add to the meat in the bowl and let cool, then stir in the feta and mint.

Divide the potato mixture into 12 portions and shape them into small patties. Place a little of the lamb stuffing in the center of each one and then reshape the potato into an oval so the filling is completely enclosed. Heat some vegetable oil to 350°F in a deep-fat fryer or a deep pot and fry the kibbeh until golden and slightly puffy. Drain on paper towles and serve.

variations

Fill the potato mixture with one of the following instead of lamb:

- *Finely chopped cooked spinach bound with cream cheese.*
- *Spicy sautéed potatoes and pitted, chopped olives.*

---

tip

I LIKE TO SERVE THE KIBBEH with a Middle Eastern-style sauce. Put ²/3 cup plain yoghurt in a saucepan and whisk until smooth. Mix 2 tablespoons of cornstarch with a little water to form a paste, add to the yoghurt, and stir continually over low heat until it is just below boiling point and the sauce thickens. Stir in a little crushed garlic and chopped mint and season to taste.

---

³/4 cup cracked wheat (bulgur)

a scant cup boiling water

1¹/3 cups mashed potato (made without any butter, milk, or cream)

1 large egg

1¹/2 tablespoons sweet butter, melted

¹/2 teaspoon ground cumin

¹/2 teaspoon ground coriander

A pinch of freshly grated nutmeg

Vegetable oil, for deep-frying

Salt and freshly ground black pepper

For the filling:

¹/4 cup olive oil

5 ounces lean ground lamb

A good pinch of ground allspice

2 tablespoons sweet butter

1 small onion, finely chopped

2 tablespoons pine nuts

¹/3 cup crumbled feta cheese

2 tablespoons chopped mint

IRAQI STUFFED POTATO BALLS

**IF YOU MAKE
SMALLER POTATO
BALLS, these can
be served as a
cocktail nibble.**

Here simple mashed potato is enlivened with feta cheese, chopped hard-boiled egg, currants, and spices, then rolled in shredded raw potato and fried until crisp. Serve with an Arabic-style salad of tomato, cucumber, and red onion, with a garlic, olive oil, and lemon dressing.

Heat the butter in a small pan, add the onion, and cook until soft and golden. Add the paprika, allspice, and cumin, and cook for 1 minute to infuse the onion with the spices. Transfer to a bowl and mix in the feta, hard-boiled egg, chives, and currants.

In a separate bowl, mix together the warm mashed potato, cornstarch and one of the eggs, then season to taste. Using wet hands, shape into balls the size of golf balls. Make a deep indentation in each one, fill with the feta mixture, and then reshape so the filling is completely covered by the potato. Chill for up to 1 hour.

Using the shredding blade of a mandoline (or a grater), shred the baking potatoes and dry in a cloth. Lightly beat the 2 remaining eggs. Remove the potato balls from the fridge, dip them in the beaten egg, and then roll them in the shredded potatoes, molding them with your hand to ensure they are well covered. Heat some vegetable oil to 325°F in a deep-fat fryer or a deep pot. Fry the potato balls in batches in the hot oil for 5–8 minutes, until golden. Remove with a slotted spoon and drain on paper towles. Serve.

2 tablespoons sweet butter

$^1/_2$ onion, finely chopped

$^1/_4$ teaspoon smoked paprika

$^1/_4$ teaspoon ground allspice

$^1/_2$ teaspoon ground cumin

1 cup crumbled feta cheese

1 hard-boiled egg, diced

1 tablespoon chopped chives

2 tablespoons currants, soaked in hot water
for 30 minutes and then drained

1$^1/_3$ cups warm mashed potato (made
without any butter, milk, or cream)

1 tablespoon cornstarch

3 eggs

2 large baking potatoes, peeled

Vegetable oil, for deep-frying

Salt and freshly ground black pepper

aloo tikki

Put the unpeeled potatoes in a pot, cover with cold water, add a little salt, and bring to a boil. Reduce the heat and simmer until tender. Drain and let cool slightly, then peel the potatoes and mash well until smooth.

Heat a dry frying pan over high heat, add the flour, and toast it for 30 seconds, until lightly coloured. Let cool, then add to the mashed potato and season with a little salt. Heat half the ghee or oil in a pan, add the cumin seeds and onion, and cook until the onion is golden. Stir in the peas, ginger, green chiles, chili powder, ground coriander and lemon juice, then add the mashed potatoes, garam masala, and fresh cilantro. Mix thoroughly, transfer to a bowl and let cool.

To make the chutney, simply place all the ingredients in a blender or food processor and blitz to a coarse purée.

Divide the potato mixture into 8 balls, then flatten them to shape into round patties. Heat the remaining ghee or oil in a large frying pan and fry the patties until golden on both sides. Serve with the chutney.

1 lb. 6oz. floury potatoes

2 tablespoons besan gram flour flour

1/4 cup ghee or oil

1 tablespoon cumin seeds

1 onion, finely chopped

1 1/4 cups peas, cooked

1-inch piece of fresh ginger root, finely chopped

2 green chiles, seeded and finely chopped

1/2 teaspoon chili powder

2 teaspoons ground coriander

1 tablespoon lemon juice

1 tablespoon garam masala

1 tablespoon chopped cilantro

Salt

For the mint chutney:

1 bunch of mint

2 plum tomatoes, cut into chunks

1 teaspoon cumin seeds

1/2 teaspoon garam masala

1 garlic clove, crushed

Juice of 1/2 lemon

1 teaspoon white wine vinegar

italian potato rissoles

If you asked me what I consider a great marriage of food, tomatoes, mozzarella, and basil would surely come to mind. I use it here for topping these delicate potato rissoles. A dish everyone will appreciate.

Place the hot mashed potato in a bowl and beat in half the butter, the egg yolk, and some seasoning. Slowly mix in the flour and Parmesan cheese, then the cream, to form a fairly stiff dough. Shape into 8 small, round rissoles.

Heat the oil and the remaining butter in a large frying pan, add the potato rissoles, and cook for 4–5 minutes on each side, until golden brown. Transfer to a baking sheet.

For the topping, place a slice of tomato on top of each rissole, then cover with the mozzarella. In a small pan, infuse the olive oil, garlic, and basil leaves over low heat for 1 minute, then spoon them over the rissoles. Season with salt and pepper and place under a hot broiler until the cheese just begins to melt.

variation

As an alternative topping, mix ¹/₂ cup fromage frais (or, if unavailable, sour cream) with 1 tablespoon each of chopped chives and dill. Place a dollop on each potato rissole, scatter ¹/₂ cup grated sharp Cheddar on top and place under the broiler until hot and bubbling.

¹/₂ cup hot mashed potato (made without
   any butter, milk, or cream)

¹/₂ stick (¹/₄ cup) sweet butter

1 egg yolk

1 cup plus 2 tablespoons all-purpose flour

1 cup freshly grated Parmesan cheese

1 tablespoon heavy cream

2 tablespoons olive oil

Salt and freshly ground black pepper

For the topping:

2 plum tomatoes, skinned and cut into 4
   slices each

1 buffalo mozzarella cheese, cut into 8 slices

1 tablespoon olive oil

1 garlic clove, crushed

8 basil leaves

ROTOLO DI patata

*In this recipe, slices of prosciutto replace the usual pasta sheets to
encompass a filling of garlicky porcini mushrooms and mashed potato. A
really flavorsome dish, served with a light balsamic butter.*

Place the unpeeled potatoes in a large pot, cover with water, add a
little salt, and bring to a boil. Reduce the heat and simmer until just
tender, then drain well. Peel while still warm and mash until smooth.
Transfer to a bowl and mix in 2 tablespoons of the butter, the egg yolk,
and the grated Parmesan.

Heat the oil in a frying pan, add the porcini, shallots, and half the garlic,
and fry for 2–3 minutes, until the mushrooms are golden and tender.
Add to the mashed potatoes and mix together. Season to taste with
nutmeg, salt, and pepper, and let cool.

Arrange overlapping slices of the prosciutto in a 12-inch square on a
piece of well-buttered foil. Spread the potato mixture over the
prosciutto in a layer about ¹/2-inch thick. Lifting the foil as you go, roll it
up neatly, making sure the potato mixture is completely covered by
the prosciutto. Refrigerate for 2–3 hours, until the roll is firm. Carefully
remove the foil and cut the roll into 12 slices.

Heat another 2 tablespoons of the butter in a large non-stick frying
pan and fry the slices until golden on both sides. Place in a serving
dish and keep warm. Clean the pan, add the remaining butter and
heat with the remaining garlic and the sage leaves until the butter is
foaming and nutty in fragrance. Stir in the balsamic vinegar. Pour the
foaming butter over the potato slices and top with the Parmesan
shavings. Serve immediately.

1 lb. floury potatoes

1 stick (¹/2 cup) sweet butter

1 egg yolk

1¹/2 cups freshly grated Parmesan cheese
    plus 1 cup fresh Parmesan shavings, for
    serving

2 tablespoons olive oil

9 ounces fresh porcini mushrooms, thinly
    sliced (about 2¹/2–3 cups)

2 shallots, finely chopped

1 garlic clove, crushed

Freshly grated nutmeg

9 ounces thinly sliced prosciutto (about
    16–18 slices)

10 small sage leaves

2 tablespoons balsamic vinegar

Salt and freshly ground black pepper

red wine-glazed potato galette with shallots, chestnuts, and lardons

Here the potatoes are glazed in red wine, so they not only taste great but also look spectacular. Port works equally well. Serve as an accompaniment to game dishes. For those with a little extra time on their hands, it is well worth making individual portions – they make a stunning presentation.

Preheat the oven to 400°F. Heat a dry frying pan until very hot, add the bacon, and sauté for 2–3 minutes, until golden and crisp. Stir in the shallots, garlic, chestnuts, and parsley, season lightly, then remove from the heat and set aside.

Heat half the duck or goose fat in an 8-inch ovenproof frying pan, then remove from the heat. Arrange half the potatoes in overlapping slices in the pan and season with salt and pepper. Top with the bacon and chestnut mixture, then cover with the remaining potatoes, arranged attractively in overlapping slices. Spoon over remaining fat over them, and season.

Cook the potatoes on the stove for about 5–8 minutes, until they start to brown underneath. Flip the galette onto a plate, then slide it back into the pan, brown-side uppermost. Continue cooking until the other side is brown. Press down with a plate to compress the potatoes, pour the wine over them, then cover with foil and cook for 10 minutes, pressing the potatoes down occasionally, until the wine has evaporated and the potatoes have taken on a light ruby color. Turn out onto a serving plate and serve immediately.

3 ounces Canadian bacon, cut into lardons (small strips)

4 shallots, thickly sliced

2 large garlic cloves, crushed

3 ounces (about 1/2 cup) frozen or vacuum-packed chestnuts, (defrosted) and chopped

2 tablespoons chopped parsley

1/4 cup duck or goose fat

1 lb. 2 oz. waxy potatoes, peeled and cut into slices 1/8-inch thick (about 3 1/2-4 cups)

1/2 cup red wine

Salt and freshly ground black pepper

perfect fries

4 large, floury potatoes

Sunflower oil or lard, for deep-frying

Coarse sea salt or Kosher salt

Peel the potatoes, rinse under cold water, and then dry on paper towles. Cut them into strips about $1/2$-inch wide by 2 to 3 inches long.

Half-fill a deep-fat fryer or deep, heavy pot with sunflower oil or lard and heat it to 300°F. Fry the potatoes in the oil in batches for 5–8 minutes, until they are soft but still very pale. Lift out and drain on paper towles (the fries can be prepared up to this stage several hours in advance, as long as the final frying is done just before serving).

Raise the temperature of the oil to 400°F and return the fries, in batches again, to the fryer. Fry for 2–3 minutes, until golden and crisp. Drain on paper towles and pile onto a hot serving plate. Sprinkle liberally with coarse sea salt and serve.

CHIPS TO BRAG ABOUT

DIPS FOR CHIPS AND FRIES

Here are my favourite dips for serving with fries:

- Mustard-smoked paprika mayo (see page 139).
- Harissa mayonnaise – simply stir harissa paste into good-quality mayonnaise until it is spicy enough for your taste.
- Tomato and fresh ginger mayonnaise – finely grate a 1/2-inch piece of fresh ginger root and stir it into 1/2 cup good-quality mayonnaise, with tomato ketchup to taste.

BARBECUE FRENCH FRIES

You won't need all the barbecue spice mix for this recipe but the rest can be stored in an airtight container for about a month. It is very adaptable and can be sprinkled over vegetables or rubbed on fish or meat before barbecuing or grilling.

4 large, floury potatoes

Sunflower oil, for deep-frying

Sea salt or Kosher salt

For the barbecue spice mix:

2 tablespoons dried red chili flakes

1 1/2 tablespoons paprika

1 1/2 teaspoons ground cumin

1 1/2 teaspoons ground coriander

1 1/2 teaspoons sugar

1 teaspoon salt

1/2 teaspoon mustard powder

1/2 teaspoon freshly ground black pepper

1/2 teaspoon dried thyme

1/2 teaspoon mild curry powder

1 teaspoon cayenne pepper

For the barbecue spice mix, put all the ingredients in a bowl and mix until thoroughly combined.

Prepare and cook the fries as for the Perfect Fries (see page 106). After the second frying, place them in a baking pan lined with paper towels to absorb excess oil, season lightly with sea salt, then sprinkle with about 2 tablespoons of the barbecue spice mix. Serve immediately.

OVEN FRIES

Okay, so you can buy oven fries in the supermarket but really, should you? This is an easy alternative to frying, with no pans full of deep fat needing constant attention. All you need is a large baking pan.

1lb. 6oz. floury potatoes

1/4 cup vegetable oil

Sea salt and freshly ground black pepper

Preheat the oven to 400°F. Cut the unpeeled potatoes into thick wedges and lay them flat in a single layer on a large cookie sheet. Pour the oil over them and toss the potatoes, then season with coarse salt and a little pepper. Place in the oven and cook for 30 minutes, by which time they should have colored on the bottom. Turn them over and continue cooking for 10–15 minutes, until they are golden and wonderfully crisp. Serve hot from the oven.

VARIATION

Orange- or white-fleshed sweet potatoes, used in exactly the same way, also make great fries.

if you think the recipes in this chapter

will err on the stodgy side, you are in for a pleasant surprise. Potatoes can add lightness to many dishes, especially breads, pancakes, and pies. Some of the pies are hearty affairs, such as the Potato, Mozzarella, and Salami Pie (page 131), but others are delicate little morsels that can even be served as canapés: try the Smoked Ham and Roquefort Kipfel (page 124) or the Potato and Salt Cod Empanadas (page 125).

Originally, adding potato to the dough when making bread was a way of making precious flour go further, but potato breads soon became prized for their light texture and good keeping qualities. Potato breads are common in many different cuisines, from the Farls and Boxty of Ireland (pages 114 and 111) to the Potato Pooris of India (page 115) and the Lefse, or flat bread, of Norway (page 117).

Potato pancakes are hugely popular throughout the world and sadly there is only room for a small selection in this chapter. They can be surprisingly sophisticated – for the ultimate light and fluffy potato pancake, try the famous Crêpes Vonnasienne on page 121, from Georges Blanc's legendary restaurant in France.

BREADS, PANCAKES, AND PIES

Basic potato bread

This versatile bread has good keeping qualities and can be used as you would any white loaf. I like it as a base for Welsh rarebit and also use it to make Cuban Bread Pudding (see page 166).

Warm the oven to 240°F. Put the yeast, half the sugar, and a little of the milk in a small bowl and mix until dissolved. Put the flour in a bowl and warm briefly in the oven. Rub in the butter, then stir in the remaining sugar, the warm mashed potato, and the salt. Pour in the remaining milk and the beaten egg, and mix to a soft, pliable dough, adding a little water if necessary. Turn out onto a lightly floured work surface and knead thoroughly for 8–10 minutes, then place in a clean bowl, cover with a cloth, and leave in a warm place for about 45 minutes or until doubled in volume.

Punch down the risen dough with floured hands, turn it out onto a floured surface, and knead for a couple of minutes. Shape into a round loaf and place on a greased baking sheet. Cover and let rise again for about 30 minutes or until doubled in size.

Preheat the oven to 400°F. Brush the loaf with a little beaten egg and bake for 25–30 minutes, until it is well-browned and sounds hollow when tapped underneath. Transfer to a wire rack and let cool.

1 ounce (about 1$^{1}/_{2}$ tablespoons) fresh yeast

3 tablespoons sugar

$^{2}/_{3}$ cup whole milk

4 cups stone-ground or white bread flour

$^{1}/_{2}$ stick ($^{1}/_{4}$ cup) sweet butter, cut into small pieces

$^{1}/_{2}$ cup warm mashed potato (made without any butter, milk, or cream)

1 teaspoon salt

1 egg, beaten, plus a little extra beaten egg to glaze

BOXTY BREAD

I found this recipe in an old cook book when travelling through Ireland. Boxty is a traditional Irish potato dish, created at a time when wheat flour was an expensive commodity so potatoes became a cheaper alternative. It can be prepared as a biscuit-like bread, as below, or thinned with milk and cooked as a pancake on a griddle. Both methods are delicious.

1/2 lb. large, floury potatoes, peeled and coarsely grated (about 1 1/2 cups)

1 cup mashed potato (made without any butter, milk or cream)

1 1/2 cups all-purpose flour

1 teaspoon baking powder

1/2 stick (1/4 cup) sweet butter, softened

1/2 teaspoon salt

Preheat the oven to 350°F. Place the grated potatoes in a thin lint-free towel or a piece of cheesecloth and squeeze out all the liquid. Place in a bowl, add the mashed potatoes, flour, baking powder, softened butter, and salt, and mix well.

Turn the mixture out onto a floured board and divide in half. Roll each portion into a circle about 1/4-inch thick and score a cross on the top. Place on a well-buttered baking sheet and bake for about 40 minutes, until browned and risen. Serve hot from the oven, broken into quarters, with lashings of butter.

fennel seed and sweet potato bread

A recipe I've had in my possession for many years. I don't know where it originates from but it's an excellent bread.

Preheat the oven to 375°F. Put the sweet potato in a roasting pan and bake for about 1 hour or until soft. Peel the potato, discarding the skin, press the flesh through a ricer of sieve, and set aside to cool.

Sift the flour and salt into a large bowl and rub in the butter until the mixture resembles breadcrumbs. Cream the yeast and sugar together and mix in 1 cup of the milk and the beaten eggs. Make a well in the center of the flour and add the sweet potato, followed by the yeasty liquid. Using first a knife, then one hand, mix to a soft dough, adding more milk if necessary. Turn out onto a lightly floured surface and knead for about 10 minutes, until the dough is smooth and elastic. Put into a clean bowl, cover with plastic wrap and let rise in a warm place for about 1 hour or until it is one and a half times its original size. Turn out onto a floured board, sprinkle on the coriander, fennel, and pumpkin seeds, and knead for 5 minutes. Shape the dough into a round loaf and place on an oiled baking sheet. Make some cuts across the top, cover with oiled plastic wrap and leave in a warm place for 15 minutes or until it has increased by one and a half times its size.

Preheat the oven to 400°F. Carefully brush the top of the loaf with egg glaze and bake for 35–40 minutes, until it is well-risen and sounds hollow when turned out of the pan and tapped underneath.

---

1 large sweet potato, weighing about 8–10 ounces

1½ lbs. stone-ground or white bread flour

1 tablespoon salt

½ stick (¼ cup) sweet butter, cut into small pieces

1 ounce (about 1½ tablespoons) fresh yeast

2 teaspoons sugar

About 1¼ cups lukewarm milk

2 eggs, beaten, plus a little extra beaten egg to glaze

3 tablespoons fennel seeds, toasted briefly in a dry frying pan

a heaped ¼ cup pumpkin seeds

2 teaspoons ground coriander

potato farls

Serve these traditional Irish farls with butter and sugar or jam, or with Ulster fry (see below).

9 ounces floury potatoes, peeled and cut into chunks (about 1³/4 cups)

2 tablespoons sweet butter, melted

¹/2 cup all-purpose plain flour

A pinch of salt

TIP

FARLS ARE BEST MADE while the potatoes are hot. If they cool down, reheat in the microwave for about 30 seconds. If you prefer, cut the rolled-out dough into individual rounds (2 inches).

Put the potatoes in a pot, cover with cold water, add a little salt, and bring to a boil. Simmer until tender, then drain well and return to the pot to dry over low heat. Mash until smooth, place in a bowl, and beat in the melted butter. Stir in the flour and salt to make a fairly soft, pliable dough. Turn out onto a lightly floured surface and roll out into an 8- to 9-inch circle, about ¹/4-inch thick. Cut into 6 wedges (farls) and cook in a hot, heavy frying pan or on a flat cast-iron griddle, without any fat, for about 2 minutes on each side, until lightly browned. Serve hot.

ulster fry

Take pork sausages, bacon, black pudding (blood sausage), tomatoes, and eggs, and prepare a traditional fried English breakfast. The eggs are best fried in the fat after cooking the bacon. Serve hot with the potato farls. A slice of caramelized apple is also good with this breakfast, although not truly traditional.

potato POORIS

TO MAKE GARAM MASALA, mix together ¼ cup ground cardamom, 1 teaspoon ground cinnamon, ½ teaspoon ground cloves, 1 teaspoon ground cumin, and 1 teaspoon ground black pepper. Store in an airtight container.

Pooris are eaten for breakfast in northern India, usually as an accompaniment to a potato-based dish. This recipe includes potato in the dough. They make an ideal accompaniment to a traditional-style thali.

Bake the potato until tender (see page 70), then peel while hot and push the flesh through a ricer or sieve into a bowl. Briefly toast the cardamom, caraway, and cumin seeds in a hot dry frying pan until aromatic and lightly colored, then stir them into the potato.

Sift the flour into a bowl and stir in the ground cumin, black pepper, garam masala, chopped cilantro, chile, and some salt. Add the potato and, using your fingertips, mix into the flour. Add the oil and knead to form a dough, adding a little warm water if the dough is too firm. Turn out onto a lightly floured surface and knead for 8–10 minutes, until smooth and elastic, then shape into a smooth ball. Put the dough back in the bowl, coat it with a little oil, cover with a damp lint-free towel and let rest for 45 minutes.

Turn out the dough and knead for 2–3 minutes, then divide into 8 balls. Flatten each one with the palm of your hand and then roll out on a floured surface into an 8-inch circle. Heat some oil in a deep-fat fryer or a deep pot to 325°F. Fry the pooris until golden, turning them occasionally in the oil and pushing them under with a wooden spoon or spatula to keep them submerged. Drain on paper towels and keep warm until all the pooris are cooked.

1 large baking potato

½ teaspoon cardamom seeds

½ teaspoon caraway seeds

1 teaspoon cumin seeds

1¼ cups stone-ground or white bread flour

½ teaspoon ground cumin

¼ teaspoon cracked black pepper

1 teaspoon garam masala (see Tip)

1 tablespoon chopped cilantro

1 green chile, seeded and chopped

2 tablespoons vegetable oil

Oil, for deep-frying

Salt

ROLLed italian potato BReaD

This stuffed bread is packed full of sunny Italian flavors. It makes great picnic food. Left unrolled, it can be cooked like a pizza.

Mix the yeast with the warm water. Sift the flour and salt into a bowl and stir in the mashed potato. Make a well in the center, add the yeast liquid, and mix to make a fairly soft dough. Turn out onto a floured surface and knead for about 10 minutes, until smooth and pliable. Place in a clean bowl, cover with a cloth, and leave in a warm place for 1–1½ hours, until doubled in size.

Punch down the risen dough and roll out to a 12- x 10-inch rectangle, about ¼-inch thick. Arrange the new potato slices over the dough, leaving a border of about 1 inch all the way around. Top the potatoes with the prosciutto, scatter the mozzarella and basil over that, then drizzle half the olive oil on top. Season with salt and pepper. Roll up the dough to secure the filling, drizzle over it the remaining olive oil and place on a greased baking sheet. Cover, and leave in a warm place for about 40 minutes, until risen. Meanwhile, preheat the oven to 350°F. Bake the bread for 30–35 minutes, until golden. Let cool before serving.

1 ounce (about 1½ tablespoons) fresh yeast

1½ cups lukewarm water

3½ cups stone-ground or white bread flour

1 teaspoon salt

⅔ cup mashed potato (made without any
  butter, milk, or cream)

For the filling:

9 ounces cooked new potatoes, sliced
  (about 1¾ cups)

5 ounces thinly sliced prosciutto (about
  1¼ cups)

5 ounces mozzarella cheese, diced (about
  1¼ cups)

10 basil leaves

¼ cup olive oil

Coarse salt and freshly ground black pepper

Lefse potato flat BREAD

This recipe comes from Norway, where it is generally prepared on festive occasions. A special grid-like rolling pin called a lefse is used, but your good old rolling pin at home will do fine. I like to serve these flat breads wrapped around some smoked salmon and a little creamed horseradish.

2 lbs. baking potatoes

2 tablespoons sweet butter

2 cups self-rising flour

Coarse salt and freshly ground black pepper

Bake the potatoes until tender (see page 70), then cut them in half, scoop out the flesh, and press it through a sieve or a potato ricer. Mix in the butter and a little seasoning, and let cool. Stir in $1^1/2$ cups of the flour, then gradually add the remaining flour to make a stiff dough (you may not need all the flour). Divide the dough into 4, then divide each portion into 4 again. On a floured surface, roll out each piece to a paper-thin disc.

Heat a flat cast-iron griddle or a large, non-stick frying pan until fairly hot and cook each disc for 1–2 minutes on each side, until patched with brown. Stack them on top of each other as you remove them from the pan, to keep them warm and soft.

pear and potato rösti with black pudding and raclette

These are not really traditional rösti but are more like a cross between rösti and latkes – the difference being that rösti are made simply with grated potato but these include some potato flour to soak up the moisture from the pear and help bind the mixture. They are topped with black pudding (blood sausage) and slices of raclette, an exceptionally good melting cheese from Valais in Switzerland and the Savoie region of France.

Cook the potatoes in their skins in boiling salted water until not quite done, then drain well in a colander. Peel the potatoes and let cool. Grate them coarsely, place them in a clean lint-free towel and squeeze out as much liquid as possible. Place the grated potato in a bowl.

Peel, core, and grate the pear, then squeeze out the moisture from it in the same way. Add to the potatoes and season to taste, then stir in the egg yolk and potato flour. Heat a frying pan until very hot, add the bacon and fry until crisp. Add to the potato mixture and mix well.

Heat half the vegetable oil in a heavy frying pan and place 8 buttered 3-inch metal rings in it (or use 4 at a time, depending on the size of your pan). Spoon the potato mixture into the rings so it is about 1/2-inch thick and cook for about 10 minutes on each side, until brown and crisp, pressing down from time to time. Remove from the pan and keep warm. Heat the remaining oil in the pan and fry the slices of black pudding until crisp and browned on each side.

Place three slices of black pudding on each rösti, top with a slice of raclette, and place under a hot broiler until melted. Serve immediately.

tip

RACLETTE CHEESE and potatoes is a traditional combination in Switzerland. For a simple but luxurious treat, just melt a generous quantity of raclette in a pan, then pour it immediately over a dish of hot boiled new potatoes and serve with pickles.

1 lb. waxy potatoes (about 4 small to medium ones)

1 ripe but firm pear

1 egg yolk

2 tablespoons potato flour (or arrowroot)

3 ounces bacon (about 6–8 strips), chopped

1/4 cup vegetable oil

24 small slices of best-quality black pudding (blood sausage)

8 slices of raclette cheese (if unavailable, use gruyère or swiss)

Salt and freshly ground black pepper

potato socca with chicken Livers à La provençale

Socca are baked chickpea pancakes, sold by street vendors in the south of France. They are tasty and easy to make. Here I have added grated potato to the basic gram flour (chickpea flour) batter.

Preheat the oven to 475°F. For the socca, cook the potatoes in a pot of boiling salted water until just tender, then drain and peel. Grate the potatoes and set aside. Put the chickpea flour in a bowl and add the water in a steady stream, whisking constantly, to create a smooth batter. Add the olive oil and season with salt and pepper. Stir in the grated potatoes.

Pour a thin layer of olive oil into a large, heavy baking pan and place in the oven until almost smoking. Pour the batter into the pan – it should be about 1 inch deep – and place in the oven. Immediately turn the oven off and place the baking pan under a very hot broiler. Cook for about 10–15 minutes, pricking any bubbles with the point of a knife as they form, until the socca is browned on top and even lightly charred in places. It should be set underneath but still soft and moist. Keep it warm while you make the filling.

Heat the olive oil in a frying pan until smoking. Add the chicken livers and cook for about 3–4 minutes, until browned on the outside but still pink in the center. Remove from the pan and keep them warm. Add the garlic, shallots, and butter to the pan and cook until the shallots are just tender. Pour in the white wine and simmer until reduced by half, then add the tomatoes, honey, and olives, and heat through gently. Return the chicken livers to the pan along with the basil leaves and some seasoning, and reheat briefly.

To serve, cut the socca into 2-inch squares and divide between 4 serving plates, then top with the chicken liver mixture.

2 tablespoons olive oil

8 ounces chicken livers

2 garlic cloves, crushed

2 shallots, diced

2 tablespoons sweet butter

$1/4$ cup dry white wine

4 ounces (about $2/3$ cup) sun-blush tomatoes (see Tip on page 89)

1 tablespoon runny honey

12 black olives

6 basil leaves

Salt and freshly ground black pepper

For the socca:

6 ounces waxy potatoes (2 small to medium ones)

1 heaped cup besan gram flour (chickpea flour)

1 cups water

2 tablespoons olive oil, plus extra for cooking

crêpes vonnasienne

SERVE THE PANCAKES topped with smoked salmon, caviar, and crème fraîche or, one of my favorites, thinly sliced carpaccio of haddock with herb mustard crème fraîche.

These fluffy potato pancakes are the signature dish of the world-renowned restaurant, La Mère Blanc, in Vonnas, near Lyons.

Place the potatoes in a pot, cover with cold water, add some salt, and bring to a boil. Cover, and simmer until tender, then drain in a colander and return the potatoes to the pot. Add the milk, and mash well, making sure there aren't any lumps. Whisk in the potato flour, then whisk in the whole eggs one at a time, followed by the egg whites. Add the cream, and season to taste. Let rest for 20 minutes before use, but do not refrigerate.

Heat a very thin layer of clarified butter in a non-stick frying pan and drop in about 2 tablespoons of batter at a time, to make little pancakes about 1/4-inch thick and 3 inches in diameter. Cook for 1–2 minutes, until golden and slightly crisp underneath, then flip over and cook for 2 minutes longer. Remove from the pan and drain on paper towles. Serve hot.

9 ounces floury potatoes, peeled and cut into chunks (about 1 3/4 cups)

1/2 cup whole milk

2 tablespoons potato flour (or all-purpose flour)

2 eggs

2 egg whites

1/4 cup heavy cream

Clarified butter, for frying (see Tip on page 153)

Salt and freshly ground black pepper

stacked potato blintzes with bacon and bananas

Here's a wonderful breakfast dish featuring the unusual combination of crisp bacon and sweet bananas.

For the blintzes, mix together the warm mashed potato and flour, then stir in the egg and egg yolk. Gradually add enough milk to make a batter that drops easily off the spoon. Season with salt and pepper. Heat the butter in a non-stick frying pan and drop in about 2 tablespoons of batter at a time to make little pancakes about $1/4$-inch thick and 3 inches in diameter (you will need 8 pancakes altogether). Cook for 2–3 minutes on each side, until golden and set, then remove from the pan and keep warm.

Peel and quarter the bananas. Heat the butter and sugar in a frying pan until lightly caramelized, then add the bananas and cook until golden. Meanwhile, fry or grill the bacon until crisp. Put half the pancakes on 4 serving plates and cover with the caramelized bananas. Top with the remaining pancakes, then the bacon. Pour the maple syrup on top and serve immediately.

2 large bananas

2 tablespoons sweet butter

1 tablespoon brown sugar

12 strips of bacon

$1/2$ cup maple syrup

For the blintzes:

$3/4$ cup warm mashed potato (made without any butter, milk, or cream)

$1 1/4$ cups all-purpose flour

1 egg

1 egg yolk

$1/2$ cup whole milk

2 tablespoons sweet butter

Salt and freshly ground black pepper

smoked ham and roquefort kipfel

Kipfel is a type of savory Austrian croissant, filled with all kinds of interesting things. I've added some potato to the dough, which acts as a great base for the ham and cheese filling. Quark cheese is often used in both the dough and the filling, but I like to add the salty tang of blue cheese, which I feel gives a better flavor.

To make the dough, put the potato in a pot, cover with cold water, add some salt, and bring to a boil. Cover, and simmer for 10 minutes, then drain and let cool. Peel the potato and grate finely.

In a bowl, mix together the quark, flour, butter, egg, nutmeg, and salt, then stir in the grated potato to make a pliable dough. Cover, and let it relax for up to 1 hour.

Meanwhile, prepare the filling. Melt the butter in a pan, stir in the flour, and cook over low heat for 1 minute. Beat in the cream with a wooden spoon, and simmer for a minute or two to make a very thick sauce. Remove from the heat and leave until lukewarm. Stir in the herbs, ham, and Roquefort, and chill thoroughly.

Preheat the oven to 425°F. On a lightly floured surface, roll the dough out into a long rectangle, 5 inches wide, and then cut it into triangles measuring about 5 inches on each side. Divide the filling between the triangles and roll up into croissants so the filling is completely enclosed. Place on a baking tray and brush with the egg and milk glaze. Bake for 25–30 minutes, until golden brown and delicious!

$^1/_2$ tablespoon sweet butter

$^1/_2$ tablespoon all-purpose flour

$^1/_2$ cup heavy cream

1 tablespoon chopped marjoram

1 tablespoon chopped parsley

5 ounces cooked smoked ham, chopped (about 1$^1/_4$ cups)

3 ounces Roquefort cheese, chilled and cut into $^1/_2$-inch dice

A little beaten egg and milk, to glaze

For the dough:

1 small floury potato, weighing about 4 ounces

4 ounces quark or cream cheese ($^1/_2$ cup)

1 cup all-purpose flour

$^1/_2$ stick ($^1/_4$ cup) sweet butter, softened

1 egg

Freshly grated nutmeg, to taste

Salt

potato and salt cod empanadas with orange and red pepper relish

First make the relish. Grate the zest from one of the oranges, then peel and segment both of them. Chop the segments, reserving the juice. Place the chopped orange, sun-dried tomatoes, roasted peppers, and garlic in a bowl, and stir in the orange juice and zest. Put the sugar and vinegar in a pan and boil for 2 minutes, then pour over the orange and red pepper mixture. Let cool.

To make the salt cod, put the cod in a small dish, cover with the sea salt, and leave for 2 hours. Wash the salt from the fish by running it under cold water, then put it in a pan along with the milk, garlic, and potatoes, and poach until the cod and potatoes are tender. Remove the fish and potatoes from the cooking liquid with a slotted spoon. Mash them together, then stir in the olive oil and enough of the milk to give a fairly firm consistency, like stiff mashed potato. Season with salt, pepper, and cayenne, and stir in the parsley. Let cool, then chill.

For the pastry, sift the flour and salt into a bowl and rub in the butter with your fingertips until the mixture resembles fine breadcrumbs. Pour in the water and bring the dough together into a ball. Cover with plastic wrap and let rest in the fridge for 1 hour.

Preheat the oven to 400°F. Roll out the dough on a lightly floured surface until it is about $1/8$-inch thick. Cut out twelve 4-inch circles and place a good spoonful of the salt cod mixture in the center of each one. Fold the pastry in half to form a semi-circle, pressing the edges firmly together. Crimp the edges with your fingers to seal, as you would with a pie crust. Place the empanadas on a baking sheet, brush with the beaten egg, then bake for 10–15 minutes, until golden brown. Serve hot, with the orange and red pepper relish.

7 ounces fresh cod fillet, without skin

$1/4$ cup sea salt

1 cup whole milk

3 garlic cloves, crushed

11 ounces waxy potatoes, peeled and cut into $1/4$-inch dice (about 2 cups)

3 tablespoons olive oil

A pinch of cayenne pepper

3 tablespoons chopped parsley

Salt and freshly ground black pepper

For the relish:

2 oranges

6 sun-dried tomatoes, chopped

4 red peppers, roasted, skinned, seeded, and chopped

1 garlic clove, crushed

2 tablespoons caster sugar

$1/4$ cup balsamic vinegar

For the pastry:

$4^1/2$ cups all-purpose flour

A pinch of salt

$1^1/4$ sticks ($2/3$ cup) sweet butter, cut into small pieces

$1/2$ cup water

A little beaten egg, to glaze

scamorza, ricotta, and spinach knishes

TIP

TO DRAIN RICOTTA CHEESE, line a colander with cheesecloth or thin cloth and place it over a bowl. Put the ricotta in the colander, draw up the cloth around it and tie into a bundle with string. Leave overnight in a cool place to drain off excess liquid.

You could describe knishes as the Jewish answer to the egg roll. They are usually filled with meat, potatoes, cheese, or chicken livers, and are served on Jewish festival days as an appetizer or canapé. Scamorza is an Italian cheese, usually smoked, and is rather like a cross between mozzarella and provolone. If you cannot find it, use provolone instead.

Put the potatoes in a pot, cover with cold water, add some salt, and bring to a boil. Reduce the heat and simmer until just tender, then drain in a colander. Return the potatoes to the pot and dry out over a low heat. Place in a large bowl and mash well. Add the scallions, 2 tablespoons of the butter, the drained ricotta, and the chopped spinach. Season to taste. Stir in the scamorza and soaked raisins, then add enough breadcrumbs to firm up the mixture. Let it cool.

Preheat the oven to 375°F. Melt the remaining butter in a pan. Lay out one sheet of phyllo pastry dough on a work surface and brush with melted butter. Top with a second sheet and brush with butter again, then top with the final sheet of phyllo. Cut the stack of phyllo into 4 horizontal sections, then cut lengthwise in half to give 8 sections. Place 2–3 tablespoons of the potato mixture on each filo section, fold in the sides, and roll up like egg rolls. Brush with the remaining melted butter and place on a lightly greased baking sheet. Bake in the oven for 10–12 minutes, until golden and crisp.

9 ounces floury potatoes, peeled and cut into chunks (1³/4-2 cups)

6 scallions, chopped

³/4 stick (¹/3 cup) sweet butter

a heaped ¹/2 cup ricotta cheese, drained (see Tip)

2 large handfulls fresh spinach, cooked and roughly chopped

³/4 cup thinly shaved scamorza cheese

3 tablespoons raisins, soaked in hot water for 30 minutes, then well-drained

A few fresh white breadcrumbs (see Tip on page 86)

3 large sheets of phyllo pastry dough

Salt and freshly ground black pepper

rustic potato, yorkshire blue, and walnut tarts

Serves 6

Heat the olive oil in a pan, add the onion and thyme, and cook for 8–10 minutes until the onion is lightly colored. Cook the potatoes in boiling salted water for 5–8 minutes, until just tender, then drain in a colander.

Put the onion, fresh thyme, potatoes, chives, cheese, walnuts, and crème fraîche in a bowl and season to taste. Place in the refrigerator until needed.

Preheat the oven to 400°F. Lay the pastry out flat on a work surface and cut it into 6 rectangles; it should be fairly thin, so if necessary roll it out a little more first. Place the rectangles on a baking sheet and divide the filling between them, leaving a $1/2$-inch border. Score the border with a criss-cross pattern and knock up the edges with the back of a knife. Bake the tarts for 20–25 minutes, until the pastry is golden brown.

2 tablespoons olive oil

1 onion, thinly sliced

1 teaspoon thyme leaves

12 ounces small waxy potatoes, thinly sliced, but not peeled (about $2^{1}/4$–$2^{3}/4$ cups)

1 tablespoon chopped chives

$1^{3}/4$ cups Yorkshire Blue cheese, cut into $1/2$-inch dice

2 tablespoons chopped walnuts

2 tablespoons crème fraîche or, if unavailabe, heavy cream

13 ounces ready-rolled puff pastry sheets

Salt and freshly ground black pepper

potato, Leek, and mustard torte

This tart has a potato and leek filling in a light cream. It is delicious, and very simple to prepare. I like to serve it with a crisp frisée salad with a hazelnut oil dressing.

Divide the puff pastry dough in half and roll out each piece into a 10-inch circle. Place on a baking sheet, prick with a fork and chill until firm.

Cook the potatoes in their skins in a pot of boiling salted water until tender, then drain well and leave until cool enough to handle. Peel the potatoes and cut them into slices 1/2-inch thick.

Heat the butter and oil in a pan, add the leeks, and cook gently for 4–5 minutes, until tender. Stir in the crème fraîche, thyme, mustard, and nutmeg and season to taste.

Preheat the oven to 200°C/400°F/gas mark 6. Arrange a third of the potato slices on one of the pastry circles, leaving a 1-inch border all around. Place half the leek mixture on top of the potatoes, then another layer of potatoes, the remaining leek mixture, and finally the remaining potatoes. Top with the second pastry circle and press lightly together. Using a very sharp knife, make vertical cuts along the pastry edges and then decorate the top by making cuts radiating in an arc shape from the center. Brush with beaten egg and milk, and bake for 35–40 minutes, until golden.

450g 1 lb. puff pastry dough

7 ounces waxy potatoes (about 2 small to medium)

1 tablespoon sweet butter

1 tablespoon vegetable oil

1¹/3 cups sliced small leeks

2 tablespoons crème fraîche (or, if unavailable, heavy cream)

1 teaspoon thyme leaves

2 teaspoons Dijon mustard

1/2 teaspoon freshly grated nutmeg

A little beaten egg and milk, to glaze

Salt and freshly ground black pepper

potato, mozzarella and salami pie

Cook the potatoes in their skins in boiling salted water until just tender, then drain and let cool. Peel the potatoes and cut them into slices 1/4-inch thick. Set aside.

Preheat the oven to 400°F. Lightly grease a 7- to 8-inch springform cake pan with a little of the melted butter. Line the pan with phyllo, letting it overhang the sides, and brush with melted butter. Add another layer of phyllo and brush with more melted butter. Repeat until all the phyllo has been used up.

Season the cooked potatoes well and arrange half of them in overlapping slices in the bottom of the dish. Sprinkle half the chopped parsley over them, then half the salami, in overlapping slices, followed by half the mozzarella. Cover with the sliced eggs. Spread the crème fraîche on top, then sprinkle a teaspoon of water over it. Add another layer of salami, then the mozzarella, sprinkle on the remaining parsley, then add a final layer of potatoes, seasoning as you go. Fold the overhanging phyllo pastry dough over the filling and brush with the remaining melted butter.

Bake for 20–25 minutes or until the pastry is golden brown and crisp. Let the pie cool slightly in the pan before turning it out onto a board. Cut into thick slices and serve hot or at room temperature. Both are equally delicious!

1 lb. 5 oz. large new potatoes

1/2 stick (1/4 cup) sweet butter, melted

12 phyllo pastry sheets

2 tablespoons roughly chopped flat-leaf parsley

4 ounces salami, thinly sliced (about 1 cup)

1 buffalo mozzarella cheese, thinly sliced

5 eggs, hard-boiled and thinly sliced

1/2 cup crème fraîche (or, if unavailable, heavy cream)

Salt and freshly ground black pepper

steak, kidney, and mushroom pie in potato pastry

I have used a flaky potato pastry to top this classic British pie. Parsnip, Potato, and Honey Mustard Mash (see page 47) makes an ideal accompaniment.

To make the dough, mix the flour and potatoes together, then rub in 1 stick (¹/₂ cup) of the butter. Stir in the iced water and bring together into a dough. Place in a bowl, cover with a cloth and let rest for 30 minutes. Roll out the dough into a 6 x 8-inch rectangle, about ¹/₄-inch thick. Dot half the remaining butter over two-thirds of it, then fold up the unbuttered third, followed by the top third. Press the edges together to seal, turn the dough 90 degrees, and roll out into a rectangle again. Dot with the remaining butter, then fold, turn the dough and roll out as before. Cover and leave in the fridge for about 2 hours.

Meanwhile, make the filling. Preheat the oven to 325°F. Season the beef and kidneys. Heat the oil in a large, heavy flameproof casserole dish (or other flame and ovenproof pan) until very hot, and seal the beef in batches (don't overcrowd the pan) until browned all over. Seal the kidneys too, then transfer the beef and kidneys to separate plates. Melt the butter in the same pan, add the onion, and fry until golden. Return the beef to the pan, add the Worcestershire sauce, and cook for 2–3 minutes. Stir in the tomato paste and mix well, then rain in the flour and cook for 3–4 minutes. Pour in the stout and stock and bring to a boil, stirring constantly, to make a sauce. Reduce the heat, cover the pan with a lid, and transfer to the oven. Cook for up to 2 hours, until the meat is tender, adding the mushrooms and kidneys about 15 minutes before the meat is ready. Adjust the seasoning, and put the mixture in a large deep pie dish, a large casserole dish, or 4 individual pie dishes.

Roll out the dough on a lightly floured surface until it is ¹/₈-inch thick and use to cover the pie dish. Brush with beaten egg, then place in an oven preheated to 375°F and cook for 30–35 minutes until golden. Let cool slightly before serving.

1 lb. 10 oz. rump or chuck steak, cut into 1-inch cubes

9 ounces veal kidneys, cut into 1-inch cubes

¹/₄ cup vegetable oil

¹/₂ stick (¹/₄ cup) sweet butter

1 onion, finely chopped

¹/₄ cup Worcestershire sauce

2 tablespoons tomato paste

¹/₂ cup all-purpose flour

1¹/₄ cups stout (e.g. Guinness)

3 cups beef stock

9 ounces white mushrooms (about 3 cups), cut in half

A little beaten egg, to glaze

Salt and freshly ground black pepper

For the potato pastry dough:

1¹/₄ cups self-rising flour

¹/₂ cup mashed potato (made without any milk, butter, or cream), at room temperature

1¹/₄ sticks (about ²/₃ cup) sweet butter, cut into small pieces

5 tablespoons iced water

pLenty of other dishes in this book can be served as main courses but the ones in this chapter defy categorization by cooking method, and some take a little extra time and effort to prepare. Many of them can be multiplied easily to serve large numbers, particularly the more homey "supper" dishes, such as Brixham Fish Pie (page 141), Irish Stew (page 153), My Favorite Cottage Pie (page 152) and Lamb and Potato Hotpot (page 155). Recipes such as these, if we take the trouble to prepare them properly, are fit for any gathering.

Other dishes in this chapter are more recognizably for "special occasions", demonstrating that potatoes make a perfect partner for luxurious ingredients. Try them in a creamy sauce with John Dory, morels, leeks, and truffles (page 137); as a fennel-scented crust for sea bass (page 140), or a replacement for rice in a risotto served with roast turbot (page 144).

Finally, potatoes really come into their own as vegetarian main courses. There are three included in this chapter, but vegetarians will find many more ideas throughout the book.

main
courses

mackerel plaki with saffron potatoes, Lemon, and tomato

Plaki is an easy-going Greek dish of fish and vegetables baked together in the oven. I like to make it with mackerel, which I consider one of the most underrated of the cheaper fish. It's appreciated more in Europe than in Britain, which is a great shame, as it has a wonderful flavor and moist texture, and is full of nutrients. It is particularly high in Omega-3 oils, which are good for coronary health.

Preheat the oven to 350°F. Heat ¼ cup of the olive oil in a frying pan, add the onion and garlic, and cook until softened. Stir in half the thyme and oregano, plus the tomatoes and olives. Then add the sliced potatoes, sprinkle the saffron over them, and add just enough water to cover. Cook gently for 5–10 minutes, until the potatoes are just tender.

Grease a large ovenproof dish with the remaining oil. Season the fish inside and out and put them in the dish. Sprinkle the remaining thyme and oregano on top and spread the potato mixture over that. Pour in the white wine, lemon juice and zest, then bake, uncovered, for 20–25 minutes, until the mackerel are cooked.

6 tablespoons olive oil

1 small red onion, cut into rings

3 garlic cloves, crushed

¹/₂ teaspoon thyme leaves

¹/₂ teaspoon oregano leaves

4 plum tomatoes, skinned, seeded and diced

16 black olives

12 ounces small new potatoes, peeled and thinly sliced (about 2 heaped cups)

¹/₄ teaspoon saffron strands

4 large mackerel, cleaned and trimmed

²/₃ cup dry white wine

Juice of 2 lemons

Zest of 1 lemon, finely grated

Salt and freshly ground black pepper

JOHN DORY WITH MORELS, LEEKS, TRUFFLES, AND POTATO SAUCE

A dish to serve when you want to push the boat out – it is expensive, but why not treat yourself occasionally? A good substitute for John Dory is Alaskan halibut.

Preheat the oven to 400°F. Cook the potatoes in boiling salted water until tender, then drain. Mash until smooth and set aside.

Lightly butter a large baking dish, season the fish fillets, and place in the dish. Bring the chicken stock to a boil in a pan, add the leeks and soaked morels, and poach for 4–5 minutes, until tender. Remove from the pan with a slotted spoon and set aside. Add the milk to the stock and then pour this mixture over the fish. Cover with lightly buttered wax paper and bake for 6–8 minutes, until the fish is just done. Remove from the oven and drain off the cooking liquid through a cheesecloth-lined strainer into a clean pan. Add the mashed potato and cream, and whisk until smooth. Cut 2 tablespoons of the butter into pieces and whisk them into the sauce a few at a time. Add the chives and season to taste.

Heat the remaining butter in a pan, add the leeks, morels, and truffle slices, and reheat gently, then season. To serve, place the fish in 4 soup plates. Pour the potato sauce over them and scatter the leek mixture on top.

6 ounces salad potatoes, peeled

4 x 6-ounce John Dory fillets (or other firm white fish)

1/2 cup chicken stock

20 young leeks, cut into 3-inch lengths

1/4-ounce small dried morel mushrooms, soaked in hot water for 30 minutes and then drained

a scant cup whole milk

1/2 cup light cream

1/2 stick (1/4 cup) sweet butter

1 tablespoon chopped chives

1 fresh or canned black truffle, thinly sliced

Salt and freshly ground black pepper

potato, zucchini, and jumbo shrimp spiedini with mustard-smoked paprika mayo

tip

TO SHELL AND DE-VEIN SHRIMP, twist off and discard the head if it is still attached, then break the shell open along the belly and carefully peel it off. Run the tip of a sharp knife along the back of the shrimp and lift out the black intestinal vein.

Soak 4 bamboo skewers in cold water for up to 1 hour (this helps prevent them burning on the grill). Meanwhile, cook the potatoes in their skins in boiling salted water until just tender (they should still be slightly firm). Drain and let cool, then cut in half.

In a bowl, whisk together the mustard, balsamic vinegar, oil, basil, and lemon juice. Drain the bamboo skewers and alternately thread onto them the zucchini, shrimp, and potatoes. Place in a shallow dish, season with salt and pepper, then pour the marinade over them and leave at room temperature for 2–3 hours. Meanwhile, mix together all the ingredients for the mayonnaise and season to taste.

Brush a ridged grill pan with a little extra oil and heat until very hot. Cook the skewers on it, turning frequently, for 8–10 minutes, until the shrimp and vegetables are charred and tender. Serve hot with the mustard-smoked paprika mayonnaise.

14 ounces small new potatoes (about 3 small to medium ones)

2 teaspoons Dijon mustard

3 tablespoons balsamic vinegar

3 tablespoons olive oil

10 basil leaves, torn

1 tablespoon lemon juice

3 zucchini, cut into slices $1/2$-inch thick

20 large raw jumbo shrimp, shelled and de-veined (see Tip)

Salt and freshly ground black pepper

For the mustard–smoked paprika mayo:

$2/3$ cup good-quality mayonnaise

1 tablespoon smoked paprika

1 teaspoon grain mustard

Juice of $1/2$ lemon

1 garlic clove, crushed

potato and fennel seed crusted sea bass

Sea bass and fennel have always had a great affinity. This crisp, fennel-flavored potato crust is perfect with the soft-textured bass.

Preheat the oven to 400°F. Bake the potatoes until nearly cooked, then remove and let cool. Peel them and grate into a bowl, using the coarse slice of the grater. Add the garlic and toasted fennel seeds, and season well.

Lightly beat together the milk and egg yolks. Season the fish with salt and pepper, then dip the top side of each fillet into the egg and milk. Dredge the top with the potato and fennel seed mixture, patting it on to make sure it sticks to the fish.

For the dressing, put the mustard, lemon juice, and vinegar in a bowl, and whisk in the olive oil. Add all the remaining ingredients, then transfer to a pan and heat gently.

Heat some olive oil in a large frying pan. When very hot, add the sea bass crust-side down and fry for 1–2 minutes, until golden. Reduce the heat and cook for a further 1–3 minutes, then turn it over and cook the other side.

Briefly reheat the cooked asparagus tips in the butter, and season to taste. Arrange on serving plates, top with the potato-crusted sea bass, and pour the warm dressing around them.

2 large waxy potatoes

1 small garlic clove, crushed

2 teaspoons fennel seeds, toasted briefly in a dry frying pan

$^1/_2$ cup whole milk

2 egg yolks

4 x 6-ounce thick sea bass fillets, skinned

Olive oil, for frying

20 freshly cooked asparagus tips

2 tablespoons sweet butter

Salt and freshly ground black pepper

For the dressing:

$^1/_2$ teaspoon Dijon mustard

1 tablespoon lemon juice

1 tablespoon champagne vinegar

$^1/_4$ cup olive oil

1 shallot, finely chopped

8 black olives, pitted and chopped

1 tablespoon chopped chives

2 plum tomatoes, skinned, seeded, and chopped

BRIXHAM fish pie

During my time on the British television program 'This Morning', I prepared this fish pie for a feature on basic British cooking. It was a great hit, especially with the camera crew who took no time at all to devour it.

Put the potatoes in a pot, cover with water, add a little salt, and bring to a boil. Reduce the heat and simmer until just tender, then drain in a colander and return to the pot. With a fork, lightly crush the potatoes, keeping them fairly chunky. Stir in 2 tablespoons of the butter and season to taste, then set aside.

Place the salmon and cod in a wide, deep pan, pour the milk over them and add the bay leaf and a few dill stalks. Bring to a boil, then reduce the heat and simmer for 3–4 minutes. Add the scallops and cook for a further minute. Remove all the fish with a slotted spoon. Strain the cooking liquid and set aside. Flake the cod and salmon into large pieces and place in a buttered 1 1/2 quart casserole dish, along with the scallops.

Preheat the oven to 400°F. Melt the remaining butter in a pan, add the onion, and cook over low heat until tender. Stir in the flour and cook for 1 minute. Remove from the heat and gradually stir in the reserved milk to form a sauce, then return to the heat and bring to a boil, stirring constantly. Simmer for 5 minutes, then add the cream and reheat gently. Stir in the chopped dill and shrimp, season to taste, and pour the sauce over the fish. Scatter the crushed potatoes on top until the fish is covered completely. Sprinkle the cheese over them and bake for 20–25 minutes, until the potatoes are golden and the sauce is bubbling.

2 lbs. floury potatoes, peeled and cut into chunks

3/4 stick (1/3 cup) sweet butter

8-ounce salmon fillet, skinned

8-ounce cod fillet, skinned

2 1/2 cups whole milk

1 bay leaf

2 tablespoons chopped dill (plus a few stalks)

6 fresh shelled scallops, cut horizontally in half

1 onion, chopped

1/2 cup all-purpose flour

1 1/4 cups heavy cream

4 1/2 ounces small cooked peeled shrimp (about 1 cup)

1 cup grated Cheddar cheese

Salt and freshly ground black pepper

fish cakes with tartare mousseline

I don't make fish cakes very often, perhaps because when I was at school they seemed to appear every day for lunch. However, when made well they can be excellent. Here's a great recipe with a good balance of potato and fish. The tartare sauce is finished with a little whipped cream to lighten it.

For the tartare sauce, stir the shallots, gherkins, capers, mustard, and some salt and pepper into the mayonnaise, then fold in the whipped cream. Keep in the fridge until ready to serve.

Place the mashed potatoes in a large bowl. Flake the cooked salmon and add to the potatoes along with the shrimp. Season with cayenne, salt, and pepper, then mix in the herbs and egg yolk. Turn the mixture out onto a floured surface and divide into 8 balls. Flatten them in to cakes, coat them in the flour, then dip into the beaten egg and finally coat with the crumbs.

Heat some vegetable oil to 350°F in a deep-fat fryer or a deep pot and fry the fish cakes for 3–4 minutes, until golden and crisp. Drain well on paper towles and serve with the creamy tartare mousseline and some lemon wedges.

a heaped cup mashed potato (made without any butter, milk, or cream)

14-ounce salmon fillet, cooked and skinned

a scant cup small cooked peeled shrimp

Cayenne pepper

2 tablespoons chopped mixed herbs, such as dill, parsley, and chives

1 large egg yolk

All-purpose flour, for dusting

2 eggs, lightly beaten

1^1/$_4$ cups panko breadcrumbs (see Tip) or, if unavailable, use ordinary dried white breadcrumbs

Vegetable oil, for deep-frying

Salt and freshly ground black pepper

Lemon wedges, for serving

For the tartare mousseline:

2 shallots, finely chopped

1 tablespoon finely chopped cocktail gherkins

1 tablespoon superfine capers, rinsed and drained

^{1}/$_2$ teaspoon Dijon mustard

^{1}/$_2$ cup good-quality mayonnaise

^{1}/$_4$ cup whipping cream, semi-whipped

baked sea bream on potato and fennel boulangère

This recipe is a play on the classic potato boulangère, where sliced potatoes and onions are baked in a flavorful stock. Here I add thinly sliced fennel, which goes particularly well with this most delicate of fish. Salsa verde makes a good accompaniment.

Preheat the oven to 400°F. Heat half of the olive oil in a pan, add the fennel and onion, and cook over low heat until soft and pale golden.

Lightly rub an earthenware casserole dish with a little oil. Arrange a layer of potatoes over the bottom, season with salt and pepper, and top with the fennel mixture. Arrange the remaining potatoes attractively on top in an overlapping layer, season, then pour the chicken stock over them so the vegetables are just covered. Dot the surface with the butter and bake for 30 minutes, until golden and crusty.

Remove the boulangère from the oven, season the fish, and place it on top of the potatoes. Drizzle over it the remaining olive oil, then return to the oven for 8–10 minutes, until the fish is done.

$1/4$ cup olive oil

2 large fennel bulbs, thinly sliced

1 onion, thinly sliced

1 lb. 5 oz. waxy potatoes (about 5 small to medium ones), peeled and cut into slices $1/8$-inch thick

3 cups chicken stock

2 tablespoons sweet butter, cut into small pieces

4 x 5-ounce sea bream (porgy) or Arctic char fillets

Coarse sea salt or Kosher salt and freshly ground black pepper

ROASTED TURBOT WITH PANCETTA, SQUID, AND POTATO RISOTTO

This unusual risotto substitutes potatoes for the rice. The squid is wrapped in pancetta, which helps keep it moist and tender.

Using a mandoline or a large knife, cut the potatoes into tiny cubes slightly larger than rice grains, placing them in cold water as you go. Cook the peas in boiling salted water, then drain, refresh under cold running water, and set aside. Heat half the olive oil in a pan, add the shallots, thyme leaves, and garlic, and sauté over low heat for 2–3 minutes. Drain the potatoes well and dry in a clean cloth. Add them to the shallots and sauté until opaque. Stir in the chicken stock, a little at a time, until all the liquid has been absorbed and the potatoes are cooked through. This should take about 15–20 minutes; do not let the potatoes become mushy. Add the cream, Parmesan, and cooked peas, and season to taste. Keep warm.

Preheat the oven to 400°F. Shred the squid lengthwise into strips about ¼-inch thick. Divide into 4 portions and wrap each portion in a slice of pancetta. Heat the butter and the remaining oil in a large ovenproof frying pan. Season the turbot and the squid wraps, place both in the pan, and cook briefly until browned on both sides. Transfer to the oven, adding the sprigs of thyme for garnish to the pan, and roast for about 3–4 minutes, until the fish is just cooked through. Remove from the oven and keep warm.

For the sauce, place the vinegar, shallots, thyme, and bay leaf in a pan, and bring to a boil. Add the red wine and boil until almost completely evaporated, then add the stock and boil until the sauce has reduced and thickened enough to coat the back of a spoon.

Arrange the potato risotto on 4 plates. Top with the roasted turbot, then with the pancetta-wrapped squid. Pour the red wine sauce around them, garnish with the thyme, and serve.

12 ounces large new potatoes, peeled

1 cup fresh or frozen peas

¼ cup olive oil

2 shallots, finely chopped

Leaves from 1 sprig of thyme, plus 4 sprigs
   of thyme for garnishing

1 garlic clove, crushed

1¾ cups chicken stock

¼ cup heavy cream

½ cup freshly grated Parmesan cheese

2 large squid, cleaned

4 large, thin slices of pancetta, weighing
   about 4 ounces in total

½ stick (¼ cup) sweet butter

4 x 6-ounce turbot fillets (if unavailable, use
   cod or Alaskan halibut)

Salt and freshly ground black pepper

For the red wine sauce:

5 tablespoons red wine vinegar

2 shallots, chopped

A sprig of thyme

1 bay leaf

⅔ cup red wine

1¼ cups meat stock

garlic braised chicken with lemon and rosemary potatoes and olives

TIP

IN ORDER FOR THE SAUCE TO FORM A GLAZE, you need to use good gelatinous stock in this recipe. Either buy one of the tubs of fresh stock now available in most large supermarkets or use home-made stock.

Preheat the oven to 400°F. Heat the olive oil and butter in a large ovenproof frying pan or a flameproof roasting pan. Add the chicken pieces in a single layer, then add the whole garlic cloves and the bay leaf, and cook for 8–10 minutes, until colored all over. Cover with foil, transfer to the oven, and bake for 25 minutes. Meanwhile, cook the potatoes in boiling salted water for 8–10 minutes, until just tender. Drain and cut into wedges 1-inch thick.

Add the wine to the pan and stir to coat the chicken pieces in it, then add the potatoes, rosemary, lemon zest, olives, stock, and some seasoning, and return to the oven, uncovered, for 15 minutes, until the sauce has formed a glaze around the chicken. Remove from the oven, add the balsamic vinegar, and toss together, then serve.

¼ cup olive oil

2 tablespoons sweet butter

12 small chicken joints

12 garlic cloves, peeled but left whole

1 bay leaf

10 ounces small waxy potatoes (about 3), peeled

5 tablespoons dry white wine

½ tablespoon roughly chopped rosemary

Zest of 1 lemon, finely grated

12 green olives

1 cup good-quality chicken stock

2 tablespoons balsamic vinegar

sausages with caramelized truffle potatoes, red onions, and garlic

A comforting meal that makes a change from the usual sausage and mash. The balsamic vinegar and wine sauce gives the sausages a delicious sweet aftertaste.

Preheat the oven to 375°F. Cook the truffle potatoes in their skins in a pot of boiling salted water until tender, then drain, refresh under cold water, and peel them while warm. Cut them in half lengthwise and set aside.

Cut the red onions into wedges, leaving the root intact. Place the red onions, potato halves, and garlic cloves in a roasting pan, pour in 6 tablespoons of the olive oil and the balsamic vinegar, then add the sugar, sage, and thyme. Roast in the oven for about 30 minutes, until tender and caramelized.

Meanwhile, heat the remaining oil in a frying pan, add the sausages, and cook for 10–12 minutes, until browned all over. Add them to the roasting pan, pour in the red wine and stock, season, and cook for 10–15 minutes, until the sausages are done.

12 ounces truffle potatoes (black potatoes)
    or, if unavailable, use purple potatoes
    (all-blue potatoes)
4 red onions
12 garlic cloves, unpeeled
1/2 cup olive oil
1/4 cup balsamic vinegar
2 tablespoons brown sugar
1 tablespoon roughly chopped sage
1 tablespoon thyme leaves
1 lb. best-quality pork sausages
2/3 cup red wine
2/3 cup meat stock
Salt and freshly ground black pepper

my favorite cottage pie

Heat the vegetable oil in a large pan until smoking, season the beef with salt and pepper, then add it to the pan and fry for 3–4 minutes, until browned (this is best done in 2 batches, so as not to overcrowd the pan). When each batch is sealed, transfer to a colander to drain off the excess fat.

Melt the butter in the pan, add the garlic, vegetables, bacon, and herbs, and cook for 3–4 minutes, until they begin to turn golden. Return the beef to the pan, add the tomato paste, and mix thoroughly. Cook over low heat for 2–3 minutes, then sprinkle in the flour, stir it in, and cook for a further 2–3 minutes. Pour in the red wine and bring to a boil, stirring as you go. Finally add the hot stock and orange zest and stir to form a sauce. Tuck in the bay leaf, cover the pan, and simmer for 1–1 1/2 hours (or cook it in the oven at 375°F), until everything is tender and a thick sauce has formed around the meat.

Meanwhile boil the potatoes and parsnips separately until tender, then drain and mash them separately. Combine them in a bowl, stir in the egg yolks, cream, cheese, and mustard, and season to taste.

Transfer the beef mixture to an ovenproof dish and let cool. Preheat the oven to 375°F. Cover the beef mixture with the potato and parsnip mash and bake for 30–35 minutes, until the top is a nice, crusty, golden brown.

1/4 cup vegetable oil

1 lb. finely minced lean beef

1/2 stick (1/4 cup) sweet butter

1 garlic clove, crushed

1 large carrot, finely chopped

1 onion, finely chopped

1 large parsnip, finely chopped

1 rutabaga, finely chopped

10–12 strips bacon, chopped

Leaves from 1 sprig of rosemary, chopped

Leaves from 1 sprig of thyme, chopped

2 tablespoons tomato paste

1/2 cup all-purpose flour

2/3 cup red wine

3 cups hot beef stock

1 bay leaf

Zest of 1 orange, finely grated

Salt and freshly ground black pepper

For the potato crust:

1 lb. floury potatoes, peeled and cut into
    chunks (about 3–3 1/2 cup)

11 ounces parsnips, peeled and cut into
    chunks (about 2 3/4–3 cups)

2 egg yolks

1/2 cup heavy cream

1/4 cup grated Cheddar cheese

1/2 tablespoon Dijon mustard

Salt and freshly ground black pepper

DRY-SPICED NEW POTATO CURRY

Cook the new potatoes in boiling salted water for 10 minutes, then drain well and set aside. In a frying pan, dry-roast the cumin and fenugreek seeds for 1 minute, until fragrant. Remove from the pan and let cool, then grind them in a mortar or blender, along with a little water, to form a paste. Heat half the ghee or clarified butter in a pot, add the onion, and fry until lightly golden. Add the remaining ghee or clarified butter, then add the curry leaves and mustard seeds and fry for 30 seconds. Stir in the paste and cook for 2–3 minutes. Add the potatoes, turmeric, coconut, red chiles, and enough water to half cover the ingredients. Cover the pot and cook gently for 8–10 minutes. Serve with fluffy plain boiled rice, preferably basmati.

1 lb. 6 oz. new potatoes, peeled

1 tablespoon cumin seeds

1 teaspoon fenugreek seeds

1/4 cup ghee or clarified butter
   (see Tip)

1 onion, chopped

8 fresh curry leaves

2 teaspoons black mustard seeds

1 teaspoon turmeric

1/4 cup dry unsweetened coconut

2 red chiles, seeded and chopped

Salt and freshly ground black pepper

IRISH STEW

I once worked with an Irish chef who insisted that potatoes should be the only vegetable in this dish. Well, being English, I have decided to express a little poetic licence and add carrots, celery, parsnip, and thyme to this renowned stew.

Arrange a layer of the lamb in a deep pot. Follow with a layer of onions, carrots, celery, and parsnip, then season lightly. Sprinkle in half the thyme and some of the parsley, then cover with a layer of potatoes. Top with the remaining meat, followed by the vegetables, seasoning, and herbs (reserve a little parsley for the garnish), then add a final layer of potatoes.

Pour in the stock and bring to a boil. Cover with a lid or foil and simmer gently for 1 1/2–2 hours (or place in a low oven). Fat from the lamb will be released to the surface, so it may be necessary to skim off a little fat as it cooks. When the stew is ready, the meat and vegetables should be tender and some of the liquid should have been absorbed by the potatoes. Sprinkle the remaining parsley on top before serving.

2 lbs. neck end of lamb, cut into chops (if
   unavailable, use shoulder or breast)

3 onions, thinly sliced

2 carrots, sliced

2 celery stalks, sliced

1 parsnip, sliced

1 teaspoon thyme leaves

2 tablespoons chopped parsley

1 lb. 10 oz. floury potatoes, peeled
   and sliced

2 cups 1/2 lamb or other meat stock
   (or water)

Salt and freshly ground black pepper

Lamb and potato hotpot

A hearty comfort food if ever there was one. This hotpot takes me back to my childhood, when it made a regular appearance on our dinner table. It originates from Lancashire, where some of the best black pudding (blood sausage) in Britain is made, and is sometimes known as tattie pot. Serve with pickled red cabbage.

Preheat the oven to 375°F. Trim excess fat from the lamb and remove the skin and central core from the kidneys.

Heat the lard in a heavy flameproof casserole dish (or other flameproof and ovenproof pot), add the lamb, and fry for 2–3 minutes, until well-sealed and golden on both sides. Remove and set aside. Add the kidneys and blood pudding and seal them on both sides, then remove from the pot.

Add the onions and half the thyme to the casserole dish and fry for 4–5 minutes, until golden. Place the meat on top, starting with the lamb, then the kidneys, and finally the blood pudding. Arrange the potatoes in overlapping slices over the blood pudding, seasoning with salt and pepper as you go. Sprinkle over it the remaining thyme leaves.

Pour in the hot stock so that the potatoes are just covered, add a final seasoning, then dot the top of the potatoes with the butter. Cover the casserole dish, transfer to the oven, and bake for 1–1$\frac{1}{4}$ hours. Remove the lid and bake for a further 30 minutes to crisp up the potatoes and give them a lovely golden color.

8 lamb shoulder neck slices (bone in)

4 lamb kidneys

2 tablespoons lard (or vegetable oil)

2 blood puddings (blood sausages), cut into $\frac{1}{4}$-inch thick

2 onions, thinly sliced

1 tablespoon thyme leaves

1$\frac{1}{2}$ lbs. baking potatoes, peeled and thinly sliced

3 cups hot meat stock

2 tablespoons unsalted butter

Coarse salt and freshly ground black pepper

sweet potato Laksa

A really satisfying noodle soup from Indonesia and Malaysia. There are many recipes for laksa, using chicken, fish, or shrimp, but this one is ideal for vegetarians. The list of ingredients may look long but it is simple to prepare.

Heat 1 tablespoon of the oil in a large pan, add the bean curd, and fry until golden and crisp. Remove from the pan and set aside.

Heat the remaining oil in the pot, add the onion and garlic, and cook over medium heat until softened. Add the sweet potatoes and toss with the onion and garlic. Stir in the ground macadamia nuts, cumin, coriander, half the chile, and the blachan, and cook for 2 minutes. Add the curry paste and cook for 5 minutes to release the fragrance. Stir in the stock and bring to a boil, then add the coconut milk, sugar, and lime zest, reduce the heat to a simmer, and cook for 10 minutes.

Cook the rice noodles in boiling water for 5 minutes and then drain. Place them in 4 deep soup bowls and top with the fried bean curd. Stir the bean sprouts into the soup, season to tase, and pour the soup over the noodles. Sprinkle the scallions, cilantro, mint, and remaining chile on top, and serve.

3 tablespoons peanut or vegetable oil

2 x 4-ounce cakes pressed bean curd (tofu), cut into $1/2$-inch cubes

1 onion, finely chopped

2 garlic cloves, crushed

12 ounces orange-fleshed sweet potatoes, peeled and cut into $1/2$-inch cubes

$1/3$ cup ground macadamia nuts

1 teaspoon ground cumin

1 teaspoon ground coriander

2 small red chiles, seeded and thinly sliced

$1/2$ teaspoon blachan (shrimp paste)

$1 1/2$ tablespoons yellow (or red) Thai curry paste

$1 1/4$ cups vegetable (or chicken) stock

$2 1/2$ cups coconut milk

1 tablespoon brown sugar

Zest of 1 lime, finely grated

9 ounces flat rice noodles

7 ounces bean sprouts (about $3 1/2$–3 cups)

4 scallions, shredded

1 tablespoon chopped cilantro

1 tablespoon chopped mint

Salt and freshly ground black pepper

Here are several of my favorite sauces for giving a kick to simply boiled or steamed potatoes. The potatoes and their sauce can be served as an accompaniment to plain roast or grilled meat or fish – although many of them are delicious enough to be served as a dish in their own right.

sauces for boiled potatoes

camembert cheese fondue

1 garlic clove, peeled

7 ounces ripe Camembert cheese, rind
removed

2 tablespoons crème fraîche or, if
unavailable, heavy cream

1 tablespoon kirsch

2 tablespoons chopped chives (optional)

Rub the inside of a small pan
with the garlic clove. Place the
cheese and crème fraîche in the
pan and heat very gently until
the cheese has melted. Stir in the
kirsch and the chives, if using,
and pour over hot potatoes.

baked potato, buttermilk, and herb dressing

1 large floury potato

1 tablespoon Dijon mustard

1 garlic clove, crushed

1 tablespoon olive oil

3 tablespoons white wine vinegar

Buttermilk

3 tablespoons chopped mixed herbs, such
as chives, basil, parsley, and tarragon

Pinch of sugar

Salt and freshly ground black pepper

Bake the potato until tender
(see page 70), then cut it in half
and scoop out the flesh into a
blender. Blitz with the mustard,
garlic, oil, vinegar, and enough
buttermilk to give a smooth,
creamy consistency, similar to
light cream. Pour into a bowl
and stir in the herbs, a good
pinch of sugar, and seasoning to
taste. Pour over hot potatoes
and serve.

shallot mustard soubise

1 tablespoon sweet butter

6 shallots, finely chopped

5 tablespoons dry white wine

2/3 cup chicken stock

1/2 cup heavy cream

2 tablespoons chopped parsley

1 tablespoon whole grain mustard

Salt and freshly ground black pepper

Heat the butter in a small pan,
add the shallots, and sweat for
5–8 minutes, until softened but
not colored. Add the wine and
simmer until it has completely
evaporated. Pour in the chicken
stock and simmer until reduced
by half. Finally add the cream and
simmer until reduced by half
again. Pour the sauce into a
blender and blitz to a purée, then
pour into a pan, reheat gently,
and stir in the parsley and
mustard. Season to taste, pour
over hot potatoes, and serve.

tip

ALWAYS ADD MUSTARD to
sauces at the last minute
and don't let it boil,
otherwise the flavor will
become bitter.

sour cream, capers, and watercress

2 bunches of watercress

1/4 cup sour cream

1 tablespoon baby capers, rinsed and
  drained

1 teaspoon finely grated lemon zest

Salt and freshly ground black pepper

Remove the stalks from the watercress and chop the leaves. Mix the watercress, sour cream, capers, and seasoning together, pour over the hot potatoes, and sprinkle with grated lemon zest.

saffron gribiche dressing

1 teaspoon Dijon mustard

1 tablespoon white wine vinegar

1/2 cup olive oil

A pinch of saffron strands, steeped in 2
  tablespoons boiling water

1 tablespoon lemon juice

2 shallots, finely chopped

2 tablespoons baby capers, rinsed and
  drained

2 eggs, hard-boiled and roughly chopped

1 tablespoon chopped parsley

Salt and freshly ground black pepper

Whisk together the mustard, vinegar, and oil. Add the saffron liquid, lemon juice, shallots, capers, hard-boiled eggs, and parsley, and mix well together. Season to taste and pour over hot potatoes.

ocopa

This Peruvian sauce, whose name dates back to the Incas, is a speciality of Lima. The recipe was given to me by a Peruvian friend who now lives in London. It is usually served as an appetizer.

4 1/2 ounces quinoa

1/4 cup olive oil

1 onion, finely chopped

1 jalapeño chile, chopped

2 garlic cloves, crushed

1 teaspoon ground cumin

2 tablespoons light soy sauce

3/4 cup grated hard cheese, such as
  Cheddar

2 tablespoons chopped parsley

a scant cup whole milk

Green olives and slices of hard-boiled egg,
  for garnishing

Salt and freshly ground black pepper

Heat a dry frying pan, add the quinoa, and dry-fry for 1–2 minutes, until lightly toasted. Pour in just enough water to cover, bring to a boil, then reduce the heat and simmer for 10–15 minutes, until the quinoa is tender and has absorbed all the water.

Meanwhile, heat half the oil in a separate frying pan, add the onion, and cook for 8–10 minutes, until softened. Stir in half the chile, the garlic, cumin, soy sauce, and some salt and pepper. Cook for a couple of minutes, then remove from the heat and let cool.

Put the onion mixture in a blender along with the remaining chile and oil, plus the cheese, parsley, quinoa, and milk, and blitz to a paste. Pour this sauce over hot new potatoes and garnish with green olives and slices of hard-boiled egg.

Jersey Royals with butter and mint

Here is a perfect example of the virtues of simplicity. Jersey Royals are one of the great tastes of summer. Until recently I was involved in the Good Food Festival in Jersey every April and May. This is when the first Jersey Royals are harvested, and what a treat they are. My fellow judges and I always looked forward to tasting them as much as to the festival itself. They are grown exclusively in Jersey, since, strangely enough, they seem to be unsuccessful anywhere else. Nothing beats their slightly sweet taste and creamy texture – it's as if the butter was grown inside them. They are at their best simply boiled or steamed, then topped with butter and mint, and no book of potato recipes would be complete without their inclusion. If you cannot find Jersey Royals, substitute using Yukon Gold or other boiling potato.

A small handful of mint

2 lbs. Jersey Royals, scrubbed

3/4 stick (1/3 cup) sweet butter

Salt and freshly ground black pepper

Bring a pot of salted water to a boil. Remove the stalks from the mint and add to the pot, along with the potatoes. Simmer for 10–20 minutes, until the potatoes are tender.

Meanwhile, chop the mint leaves and beat them with the butter in a bowl. Drain the potatoes in a colander, then place them in a serving bowl. Season to taste, top with the mint butter, and serve.

Salmorreta sauce

This sauce can be blitzed to a smooth purée, or combined roughly for a chunkier presentation

12 ounces ripe but firm plum tomatoes (about 2–3 medium ones), cut in half

1/2 teaspoon red chili flakes

2 garlic cloves, chopped

1 tablespoon chopped parsley

1 tablespoon chopped tarragon

1 red onion, finely chopped

About 1/2 cup olive oil

2 tablespoons white wine vinegar

A pinch of sugar

Salt and freshly ground black pepper

Put the tomatoes on a baking tray in a single layer and place under a hot broiler for 3–4 minutes on each side, until slightly charred. Carefully peel off the skin and discard the seeds.

Put the chili flakes, garlic, parsley, and tarragon in a mortar and crush. Add the onion and the tomato flesh and crush again. Drizzle in enough olive oil to give a pesto-like consistency, stirring constantly, then add the vinegar and sugar. Season to taste. Pour over hot potatoes, and serve.

Hot paprika and almond dressing

1 garlic clove, chopped

1/3 cup whole blanched almonds

1/4 teaspoon cayenne pepper

1/4 teaspoon hot paprika (or chili powder)

1 tablespoon sherry vinegar

1/4 cup olive oil

1 tablespoon chopped parsley

1 tablespoon chopped oregano

Salt

Whizz the garlic and almonds to a fine paste in a small food processor (or crush them in a mortar if you are feeling energetic). Transfer to a bowl and mix in the cayenne and paprika. Stir in the vinegar and olive oil, followed by the herbs, then season with a little salt. Pour over hot potatoes, and serve.

potatoes are so adaptable that

they can even be used in desserts. They add lightness and moisture to all sorts of sweet dishes, and can replace suet or a proportion of the flour in steamed and baked puddings, pastry, and some cakes. Orange-fleshed sweet potatoes, with their honeyed, almost caramelized flavor, are a natural when it comes to desserts. Don't be tempted to substitute white-fleshed sweet potatoes, though – their taste and texture are not the same at all.

This chapter contains just a few ideas for potato desserts but gives a fair indication of their versatility. Chunky Orange Marmalade Tart (page 164) includes a little mashed potato in the pastry dough for a light, soft texture. Stuffed Almond Crêpes with Peach Brandy Sabayon (page 173) rely on potatoes to produce delicate, thin crêpes. And grated potato is the secret ingredient in Steamed Lemon and Apricot Pudding (page 171). Other recipes, such as Cuban Bread Pudding (page 166), are based on potato bread. Ordinary bread can be substituted but potato bread has a unique flavor and texture that add an indefinable quality to these dishes – it would always be my first choice for making them.

a few
sweet
ideas

CUBAN BREAD PUDDING WITH BANANAS AND RUM CARAMEL

A Cuban-inspired pudding made to a lighter recipe than the original. It is flavored with coconut milk and sweet spices and topped with bananas and a rum caramel. Serve with lashings of thick cream if, like me, you don't count calories!

Preheat the oven to 325°F. Lightly grease four 6-ounce ramekin dishes. Divide the diced bread between the dishes and sprinkle the soaked raisins on top.

Put the cream, coconut milk, spices, and almond extract in a pan. Slit open the vanilla bean and scrape out the seeds into the pan, then place over a gentle heat and bring just to a boil. Meanwhile, put the eggs and sugar in a bowl and whisk until pale. Strain the cream mixture and gradually pour it into the egg and sugar mixture, whisking constantly. Pour into the ramekins and let stand for 30 minutes. Place the dishes carefully in a roasting pan and pour enough boiling water into the pan to come halfway up the sides of the dishes. Bake for 20–25 minutes or until just set, then remove from the oven and let cool slightly.

For the rum caramel, spread the sugar over the bottom of a heavy pan and cook over medium heat until melted, stirring gently from time to time so it melts evenly. Raise the heat and cook to a dark amber caramel. Cool slightly and stir in the rum.

Turn the puddings out of the ramekins and place on serving plates. Peel the bananas and cut into ¹/₄-inch thick slices. Arrange the slices of banana on top and pour the rum caramel over them.

5 slices of Potato Bread (see page 110), cut into ¹/₂-inch cubes

1 tablespoon golden raisins, soaked in hot water for 30 minutes and then drained

²/₃ cup heavy cream

1¹/₂ cups unsweetened coconut milk

A small pinch of saffron strands

¹/₄ teaspoon ground cinnamon

A pinch of freshly grated nutmeg

¹/₄ teaspoon almond extract

¹/₂ vanilla bean

3 large eggs

a heaped ¹/₂ cup sugar

2 small, ripe bananas

For the rum caramel:

¹/₂ cup sugar

¹/₄ cup dark rum

deep-fried stuffed apricots

An unusual way of serving one of my favorite and most delicate of fruits. It's also a great way of using up leftover potato bread, should you have any!

Blanch the apricots in boiling water for 1 minute, then drain well and peel off the skins. Carefully cut down one side of each apricot and remove the pit, without damaging the flesh. In a bowl, mix together all the ingredients for the filling and use to stuff the apricots, closing them up afterwards.

Stir the orange zest into the yoghurt and chill until ready to serve.

Mix together the breadcrumbs and ground almonds. Dip the stuffed apricots in the beaten eggs, then roll them in the breadcrumb mixture.

Heat some vegetable oil for deep-frying to 350°F and deep-fry the apricots for about 2 minutes, until golden – they will bob up to the surface, so keep pushing them down to let them color evenly. Drain on paper towles and serve immediately, with the orange-scented yoghurt.

12 ripe apricots

1 teaspoon finely grated orange zest

1/2 cup thick, whole milk yoghurt

3 cups fresh breadcrumbs, made from Potato Bread (see page 110)

2/3 cup ground almonds

2 eggs, beaten

Vegetable oil, for deep-frying

For the filling:

12 fresh dates, pitted and roughly chopped

1/4 cup ground almonds

Juice of 1/4 lemon

Zest of 1 orange, finely grated

1/2 teaspoon ground cinnamon

1 tablespoon orange-flower water (optional)

2 tablespoons dark rum

steamed lemon and apricot pudding

A fantastically warming winter pud, crammed with dried apricots and topped with apricot jam. Because the grated potato keeps it moist, it's surprisingly low in fat – unless you serve it with thick cream or lashings of custard sauce, as I do!

Sift the flour into a bowl, add the melted butter, then stir in all the remaining ingredients except the apricot jam. Transfer the mixture to a greased 1 quart ovenproof bowl, cover with wax paper or foil, and tie with string to secure. Place the bowl in a steamer or in a large pan containing enough boiling water to come halfway up the side of the bowl. Cover and steam for $1^1/4$–$1^1/2$ hours, topping up with more boiling water if necessary during cooking.

Remove from the pan and let cool for a few minutes, then remove the paper or foil and run a knife around the sides of the pudding to loosen it. Turn out onto a plate. Heat the jam with $^1/2$ cup water to form a sauce, then strain through a wire mesh strainer. Pour it over the pudding and serve immediately.

$^1/2$ cup self-rising flour

$^1/2$ stick ($^1/4$ cup) sweet butter, melted

$1^1/2$ tablespoons sugar

1 tablespoon corn syrup

$2^1/2$ cups soft white breadcrumbs

$^3/4$ cup grated raw potato

2 teaspoons finely grated lemon zest

$^1/2$ cup whole milk

$^1/2$ cup chopped dried apricots

$^3/4$ cup apricot jam

Stuffed almond crêpes, waiting to be covered with brandy sauce and returned to the oven for glazing

stuffed almond crêpes with peach brandy sabayon

It's a shame that in England crêpes are usually reserved for Shrove Tuesday, and rarely seen on menus. Here's one of my favorite ways to prepare them.

First make the crêpes. Put the potatoes in a pot, cover with cold water, add a pinch of salt, and bring to a boil. Reduce the heat and simmer until tender, then drain well and mash to a purée. Let cool. Mix in the eggs, then sift in the flour, add the sugar, and mix well. Gradually stir in enough milk to make a smooth, runny batter.

Heat some clarified butter in a 9-inch non-stick frying pan, add a little of the batter, and swirl it around the pan to coat the bottom thinly. Cook until golden underneath, then flip over and cook the other side. Make 8 pancakes in all, adding more butter to the pan as necessary.

For the filling, whisk the egg yolks and confectioners sugar together until creamy, then stir in the ground almonds and cinnamon. In a separate bowl, whisk the egg whites until stiff, then gradually whisk in the sugar. Gently fold the egg whites into the almond mixture. Divide the filling between the pancakes and roll them gently. Place on a large buttered baking sheet in pairs, leaving a good-sized gap in between.

Preheat the oven to 350°F. For the sauce, place the egg yolks, sugar, wine or champagne, and peach brandy in a large bowl and set it over a pan of barely simmering water (or use a double-boiler), making sure the water isn't touching the bottom of the bowl. Whisk with a hand-held electric beater until the mixture becomes light and airy and increases by about four times its volume. Fold in the whipped cream.

Pour the sauce over the pancakes and place in the oven to glaze for 5 minutes. Meanwhile, heat the 1 tablespoon butter in a large frying pan, add the sugar and cook until it forms a light caramel. Add the nectarine slices and cook until caramelized. Arrange the crêpes on 4 serving plates, garnish with the nectarines, and dust with confectioners sugar.

2 egg yolks

1 tablespoon confectioners sugar, plus extra for dusting

1 cup ground almonds

1/4 teaspoon ground cinnamon

2 egg whites

2 tablespoons sugar

1 tablespoon sweet butter

2 ripe but firm nectarines, pitted and thinly sliced

For the crêpe batter:

9 ounces floury potatoes, peeled and cut into chunks (about 1 3/4 cups)

4 eggs

1 heaped cup all-purpose flour

1 tablespoon sugar

1 cup whole milk

2 tablespoons clarified butter (see Tip on page 153)

For the sauce:

3 egg yolks

2/3 cup sugar

1/2 cup sparkling white wine or champagne

1/4 cup peach brandy

1/2 cup heavy cream, semi-whipped

INDEX

acknowLeDgements

I gratefully acknowledge the assistance of the following people, without whom this book would not have been possible.

All at Kyle Cathie especially to Kyle, and to Sheila Boniface for her help and guidance.

Jane Middleton for another superb job of editing my recipes.

Linda Tubby and Gus Filgate, food stylist and photographer, between them they make a most talented and formidable pairing – thank you.

Penny Markham, for her wonderful props, once again.

Heidi Baker for her fantastic book design.

My wife, Anita, and daughter, Lauren, for their help and PC skills during the book's initial concept.

Eddie from Laxeiro for inspiration from his wonderful Spanish recipes.

Alan Wilson, author of *The Story of the Potato*, whose help with detailed research has been invaluable.

Fiona, Linda, and Honey at Limelight for their tireless support and friendship.

To all at Chef's Connection, vegetable purveyors, for supplying excellent quality potatoes and other wonderful produce to work with.

To Mr. Geoffrey Gelardi and my team at the Lanesborough for their constant support and encouragement during the writing of this book.